Best Regards -

Billy Henderson

# THE WINNING EDGE

Stroud & Hall Publishers
P.O. Box 27210
Macon, Ga 31221
www.stroudhall.com


Printed in the United States of America
First Edition

The paper used in this publication meets the minimum requirements
of American National Standard for Information Sciences—
Permanence of Paper for Printed Library Materials.
ANSI Z39.48–1984. (alk. paper)

*Library of Congress Cataloging-in-Publication Data*

Hammack, Aubrey.
The winning edge : lessons from Billy Henderson / by Aubrey Hammack.
p. cm.
Includes bibliographical references and index.
ISBN 978-0-9796462-6-3 (pbk. : alk. paper)
1. Henderson, Billy, 1928
2. Football coaches—United States—Biography.
3. Football—Coaching—Anecdotes.
I. Title.
GV939.H46H36 2011
796.332092—dc22
[B]
2011008782

---

# THE WINNING EDGE

## LESSONS FROM BILLY HENDERSON

Aubrey Hammack

# CONTENTS

# DREAM THE IMPOSSIBLE DREAM

## "Reach for the Stars"

I am honored that Aubrey Hammack asked me to participate in the writing of his tribute book about Coach Henderson titled *The Winning Edge.*

This is a story of my thoughts and remembrances of my association with Coach Billy Henderson, the greatest coach that ever lived. This story is by no means unique. Every player ever associated with Coach Henderson has their own story to tell. I am certain that many of those stories would be more compelling than my own. I am one of many thousands that have been blessed to have been a part of Coach's life.

Coach Henderson was a natural born leader. In my view it was his destiny in life to be a Coach. I have talked to some of his teammates at old Lanier, and they remembered that, even in his youth, Coach Henderson would take his teammates aside and coach them and encourage them. He especially migrated to the younger guys who were tasting varsity competition for the first time. He loved it! He still does! He has always and always will be a Coach.

Many years have passed since, as a teenager of fourteen, I met Billy Henderson for the first time. The meeting was a happen-chance meeting that occurred on an early August night in 1958 as I pulled into the parking lot of Dairy Queen located on Houston Avenue in old South Macon. As I dismounted my motorcycle, I saw and recognized Coach Henderson standing at the service window. He was purchasing ice cream cones for his family, who were sitting in a black Chevrolet coupe close by. The children in the back seat were excited about their ice cream.

That meeting has been chronicled by others, so I will not go into details except to say that Coach Henderson introduced himself and invited me to try out for the Willingham Ram football team that was departing for football camp the next morning. Having just failed the ninth grade at Lanier Junior High School the previous school year because of a lack of attendance, I was excited that Coach Henderson had noticed me. He convinced me that a skinny 145-pounder could make a contribution in football. I had not been a bad kid at that time, but I did have a lack of structure and guidance in my life. I was definitely spiraling toward a life of failure. In fact, I had already fallen through the cracks. After meeting Coach Henderson, I went home, packed my clothes in a paper bag, and I was at Willingham High School the next morning at 7:30 A.M. ready to go!

The title of Aubrey's tribute book to Coach Henderson is *The Winning Edge*. I will attempt to speak to that title from the perspective of one of his players and as one of his former assistant coaches. In doing so, I am attempting to speak on behalf of all the Rams that put on the pads and did battle under his leadership.

A few of the early lessons Coach Henderson imparted to me in the beginning of our relationship were:
1) Don't drop your head and look down. Always hold your head up, look up.
2) He taught me how to properly shake another man's hand and to look him dead in the eyes when doing so.
3) He also emphasized that once you have made a commitment to start something, don't quit. Always finish what you start. Don't let others down, don't let yourself down. Besides, he believed that every time someone quit something, it became easier to quit the next time things got hard. No one really respects a quitter.

Coach Henderson stressed these values because he thought they were important in the development of, not only good athletes, but also in the development of good citizens. I do, too!

Most knowledgeable observers will agree that the Rams defeated many teams that had better pure athletes than did the Rams. The victory over Lanier in 1960 is cited as a case in point. What a lot of folks couldn't figure out is how they were able to do it. The truth is simple, really. Our opponents sometimes had better *athletes* but we had better *football players.* Believe me, as a coach of thirty-seven years, I know the difference. Good football players win championships. Coach Henderson and his staff knew how to develop good football players. They knew what it took to develop the ***Winning Edge***.

Coach Henderson has told me many times that there were no secrets to having success in athletics. He believed that success came about as a result of HARD WORK. If Coach Henderson didn't have work to do, he would think of something to do. He was always searching for ways to make things better.

In the summer of 1960, I once drove up to the school to find Coach Henderson for some reason or another. I can't remember the reason, but what I do remember is that Coach Henderson was not in his air conditioned office having his normal morning cigar break. I looked outside and saw him on the practice field running fifty-yard wind sprints. It was probably 100 degrees that day. A Valdosta gnat would have had a hard time breathing the air. No one was there to praise him or cheer him on. Yet he kept running fifty-yard sprints over and over. He punished himself. Realizing that he wouldn't be coming back to his office for a while, I went down to the field where he was running. I asked him, "Coach, what in the world are you trying to do, kill yourself?" His reply was, "No, but in a few weeks I will be asking my players to do this, and I don't want to ask them to do anything I haven't done."

Coach Henderson's motor never stopped running and he didn't want yours to stop either.

Nobody outworked Coach Henderson and his staff. You will have to have played under Coach Henderson to understand what he put his players through in practice. It was tough and demanding and, in my view, it is what led to his players acquiring the ***Winning Edge***.

His former Ram players will fondly remember:

1) The Board Drill
2) The Helmet Drill
3) The Moultrie Drill
4) The Ram Drill
5) The Ram Plus Drill
6) All the times Coach Henderson sent us back to the dressing room after an hour of what we thought had been a hard, productive practice, telling us practice was starting over from the beginning. Coach Henderson would literally send us all the way back to the gym and make us come back out to take the field and start practice afresh. We complained under our breath but never out loud and within ear shot of a Ram coach.

It was Coach Henderson's way or the highway. He demanded hustle and enthusiasm. Coach Henderson demanded 110% effort from those desiring to be called a Ram. After we gave him that 110%, we were proud to be Willingham Rams. It was real!

7) No Ram will forget the times Coach Henderson put the ball on our own one-yard line and made us drive the football ninety-nine yards without making a mental mistake. Some of us believed that he would always instruct

Coach Martin Allman beforehand to find a mistake before we got to the other end zone. After some fictitious off-sides penalty had been called by Coach Allman, the team was marched back to the one-yard line to start the drive over again, and again, and again.

8) Rams will too remember the agony they suffered at Willingham football camps held at Camp Perry in Lawrenceville, Georgia and in later years at Jekyll Island, Georgia. Believe me—we didn't go there for the mountain views or to hear the roar of evening tides. We went there to work. It was hard and only the strong survived. It was a process of natural selection. Some folks hid under the canvas of the ice truck when it made its daily delivery to escape the torment of football camp.

In 1959, at Camp Perry, Coach Henderson instructed his assistant coaches to put on full pads and scrimmage with the Rams' football team. All Rams' assistant football coaches strapped on the Rydells and brought it to us. Coaches Mike Garvin, Billy Beale, Dave Hill, Martin Allman, Mack Edwards, Bobby Brown, Henry Middlebrooks and Johnny Stallings played in the scrimmage and were very worthy opponents.

I had to tackle Coach Johnny Stallings once on a play near the sideline. It hurt me all over. Coach Stallings was the hardest man to bring down that I ever tried to tackle, either in high school or in college. Dave Hill looked like a round Sherman Tank in a football uniform, and Coach Billy Beale, as quarterback, looked like he was back at Georgia directing the Dogs.

I suspect a Willingham Ram football camp was very similar in nature to the one Bear Bryant put the Texas A&M Aggies through in the desert his first year there as head coach. I am not joking! Once one had played and practiced under what I now jokingly refer to as "Billy Ball," the games seemed easy. Practice was harder than the games.

Aubrey asked me if I had played one game under Coach Henderson that stood out among the others in my memory. In my mind there is no question but that it was the 13-6 victory over the mighty Lanier Poets in 1960. Lanier was the team we had cheered for as children in elementary school before there was a Willingham High School. Their reputation and athletic accomplishments were impeccable.

One had to have been from South Macon and have played in the game to fully understand it. The Saturday morning after the game, the sun seemed to shine a lot brighter on the homes lining Houston Avenue and all the side streets that connected into it.

After the victory over Lanier, a generation of Rams acquired a new sense of self-esteem, self-respect, and a confidence in themselves that would last a lifetime. I believe for the first time that Coach Henderson was able to convince Brother Jimmy Waters, pastor of Mable White, that winning was important. After the victory over Lanier in 1960, the door opened like a flood gate. In the years that followed, the Rams went on to defeat all the power house teams in Georgia including: Columbus, Albany, LaGrange, Moultrie, and Valdosta. Victories over Lanier became routine.

Those days in the '60s were the glory days of the Willingham Rams. But as good as they were, greater days lay ahead for Coach Henderson. His star was still on the rise.

In 1967, after four years of college football and with a Master's Degree in hand, I had the pleasure of serving on Coach Henderson's varsity football staff. It was my first job as a teacher and coach.

Coach Henderson would often begin our coaches' meetings by having a staff member read the Optimist Creed aloud. This document was almost like sacred scripture to him. He was a true believer in the positive outlook on life that was emphasized in the creed. He lived by this creed all his life.

In our coaches' meetings, he would sometimes, as a change, have us listen to Frank Sinatra's version of "The Impossible Dream." He got real excited when listening to this song. When the song reached the part where Sinatra sang about "reaching for the stars," Coach Henderson would raise his hand high above his head as if reaching for a star and pulling it down to himself.

As a cocky twenty-two-year-old I wasn't very impressed. Little did I know what an idiot I was at the time. I was sitting at the feet of greatness and didn't fully realize or appreciate it. I learned long ago that Coach Henderson's visions of life were always larger, purer, and more defined than my own. Coach always saw the potential for good in everyone he encountered. He always strove for the greater good in life's situations. He was a peacemaker.

Coach Henderson was not a taker. He was a giver, a servant. Worldly goods and the accumulation of wealth were never important to him. What was important to him were *people*. That is what this man was all about, family and friends.

Coach Henderson made everyone around him aspire to be all they could be. In many cases, they often exceeded their potential, myself included. I don't think there is a Willingham Ram still living that wouldn't agree with this statement.

However, let me be clear! Coach Henderson was not just a dreamer of dreams who went around staring at the clouds all day. He believed that it could be done and he went to work to make sure it was done. Coach Henderson was above all, a *man of action.* He was both a dreamer and a king-maker. Few have the gift to do both. Coach Henderson did!

In 1970, Coach Henderson bid farewell to the Rams and joined Coach Mike Garvin's staff at Mount de Sales. With his son Johnny Henderson at quarterback, Mount de Sales forged out a couple of State championships. In 1973, Coach Henderson accepted the head football job at Clarke Central High School in Athens, Georgia. He literally attacked a situation most coaches didn't want any part of. The program at Clarke Central was in the midst of a lot of turmoil.

Coach Henderson mustered all of his natural gifts and talents and threw himself into the situation. He quickly restored a belief in what it meant to be a Clarke Central Gladiator. All Gladiators were equal, in the eyes of Coach Henderson, just as the Rams had been in Macon. The best players played. That was it, end of story.

His players and the community loved him, trusted him, and believed in him. Pretty soon they were following him around like the Pied Piper, just as they had done in Macon during his glory years at Willingham.

At Clarke Central, the T-formation gave way to a multiplicity of innovative offensive and defensive schemes. Coach Henderson had the flexibility to change with the times. However, one thing remained constant in "Billy Ball." Coach Henderson worked their butts off. He outworked his opponents. His weight program was second to none in Georgia. It is easy for coaches to say that they outwork their opponents. It sounds good. But in reality, it is hard to really do it! Coach Henderson and his Gladiators did it.

During the years that followed, state championships and national championships filled the trophy cases at Clarke Central. Clarke Central became known as the School of Champions across Georgia and the Nation.

After a long coaching career that spanned more than forty years, Coach Henderson retired with honors. Rest, golf, and relaxation were not in the picture for Coach Henderson as his beloved Fosky became ill and eventually disabled. During nearly a decade of illness, Coach Henderson was by her side 24 / 7, just as she had been by his in all his years as a player and coach. Coach Henderson has also had some physical setbacks but he is still independent. His physical skills have diminished some with age but he still has that gleam in his eye that makes chill bumps run up and down your spine.

One thing for sure, Coach Henderson was not what former LaGrange coaching legend, Coach Oliver Hunnicutt, called in derision "a clip board coach," a term Coach Hunnicutt used to imply that a coach was a pretender, a coach wanna be, not a real coach. Coach Henderson was the real deal. What he had as a coach all came from within, from the heart. He was a *Coach* in the truest sense of the word, from the hair on his head to the soles of his feet as he used to say. Coach Henderson gave honor, respect, and reverence to the word *Coach.*

Early in my coaching career, Coach Henderson told me that, "having love in your heart was the most important thing in a man's life." It is something I have never forgotten. He was right. It is and always has been the most important thing in any person's life. The athletic careers don't last long. The days of career building eventually fade and are over as well. What is left after this is what mattered through the journey, *people*, both family and friends.

I don't talk to Coach Henderson often, but when I do, the first words to come out of his mouth are, "I love you like a daddy, like a brother, like a friend, and any other way you can think of." His words warm my heart and lift me up. They make me feel like I am somebody. This is the strength of the man they call Coach Billy Henderson. He affects everyone that way.

I hope my words of tribute to Coach Henderson have given insight into the man that he is and to the personal attributes that led to his greatness.

As a sixty-seven year old man, I have had a lifetime to reflect on my association with Coach Henderson and the influence that he had on my life. As a teenager, I hung on his every word just as all my teammates did, but I lacked the maturity and understanding to appreciate how fully he was guiding and influencing me.

Looking back in hindsight, I can see that he molded me just as surely as a potter molds a vessel of clay. In retrospect, I can see clearly that, day after day, he was shaping my character, my values, my attitude, and my goals in life. It was not a coincidence. It was a deliberate effort on his part. I was not alone. He was doing the same with all my teammates. I am sure it was hard work. But that's what he did.

Coach had a gift of knowing what you needed and giving it to you when the occasion arose. Sometimes it was a kick in the butt, sometimes it was to wipe the tears and let you know that he cared. Coach knew what was important in life.

In my concluding remarks, I would like to say that, no matter where he coached, Coach Henderson cast a giant shadow. He is a hard act to follow.

He is a one-of-a-kind guy. He is special. In the minds of the Willingham Rams, and I suspect in the minds of the Cavaliers and Gladiators as well, Coach Henderson is the greatest coach to ever put on a whistle and a pair of coaching shoes. If you didn't know him personally but wanted to know more about him, I hope this gives you a glimpse into the characteristics that made him successful and loved by many.

To those of us who had the privilege to have been a small part of his very large life, I hope my thoughts have revived some dear memories for you of the time you spent with Coach Henderson.

Speaking for myself and on behalf of all Willingham Rams, I say, thank you, Coach Henderson, from the bottom of our hearts. You are our Number One Everything.

May God bless you forever!

—***Jimmy Hammond***
Willingham Ram football player and coach

# INTRODUCTION

The first time I remember hearing the name Billy Henderson was in the fall of 1960. My family had moved from Thomaston, Georgia, and I had transferred from Robert E. Lee Institute to Willingham High School as a tenth-grader. I was a huge football fan growing up in Thomaston, so at Willingham, of course, I embraced the football team, just like any other kid would have done.

In the PE classes, I would see Coach Henderson every day, along with the other coaches, such as Dave Hill, Johnny Stallings, Mack Edwards, Jessie Duckworth, Martin Allman and Mike Garvin. But it was always Coach Henderson who caught my eye. He had this way of talking that just made you sit up and listen, and you always knew he was in charge. Looking back, I realize that he had charisma, though at that time, I am not so sure I knew what that word meant. Though I never played for Coach Henderson, I was one of the biggest fans of the Willingham Rams, never missing a home game.

I shall never forget that in my senior year, one day in PE, someone let out a curse word. Coach Henderson immediately asked, "Who said that?" As I was standing by friend of mine, David Renfroe, someone jokingly pointed to me. Coach Henderson came to me immediately and asked me to bend over and touch my ankles. He struck me a couple of times, and I remember hardly being able to sit the rest of the day. I didn't say the curse word, but you have to remember, in that day, you didn't question a teacher when they told you to do something.

Another incident that stands out in my mind was in the early '70s when I was doing play-by-play football for WNEX Radio in Macon. Coach Henderson, who was coaching at Mount de Sales, was in the press box, and I asked him if I could interview him at half-time. He consented and I found out how much I revered him as, during that interview, I was so nervous that my voice shook.

Later, in the '90s, while I was doing a television program for Cox Cable called "Keeping in Touch," Coach Henderson consented to do three interviews about his life in coaching. One of these was on the death of his son, Brad. I was later told by Cox Cable that those interviews were some of the most popular ones that I had done in eight years of doing that show. They reported numerous calls about them. The transcripts from those shows will be included in this book.

It was during that time that Coach Henderson first mentioned to me the possibility of writing a book on his life. A short while later, he called to say that a writer in Athens was working on a book and asked if I would contribute. I agreed. The book at that time was not completed, and later, Ed Grisamore wrote one. After that book was published, Coach Henderson talked with me about writing another book because he felt like he had more to say. He wanted to talk about the factors that led to winning, and he wanted the title to be *The Winning Edge*. In the summer of 2010, shortly after the death of his wife, Fosky, Billy and I agreed to work on this endeavor.

This book is based almost entirely on the words of Coach Henderson and the words of his family, former players, fellow coaches, and friends. Many interviews were conducted and e-mails exchanged to garner the information. In talking with all of these people, several things emerged that could be seen as being part of the winning edge. I have attempted to categorize the remarks based on these, although often certain characteristics overlapped, while others were difficult to define.

Some of these components are the more obvious things: talent and desire, preparation and organization, hard work and physical training, discipline and high expectations, teamwork and team building, and parent and community involvement. Just as important, however, are some characteristics which Coach Henderson possesses and which he has always worked at instilling in his players: motivation, positive attitude and enthusiasm, perseverance and determination, and spiritual values and compassion.

One chapter will speak to Coach Henderson's legacy and the tremendous amount of respect that others have for him. His legacy continues on indirectly, through his former players and coaches. I have an example of that in my own life—my son, Stephen Hammack, played football at Mt. de Sales Academy under Coach Mike Garvin (coach at Willingham in the 1960s), and my daughter, Karen Hammack (Petty), was co-manager of the boys basketball team at Mt. de Sales under Coach Robert Slocum, who played baseball for Coach Henderson in the 1970s. Also, because the death of Brad Henderson had such impact on so many and was referred to so often, I have included a chapter about memories of him.

Coach Henderson is, without a doubt, one of the most beloved sports figures in this state. It seems almost everyone has heard of his abilities as a coach and player, especially when it comes to football and baseball. He has left his mark on everything and everybody he has touched, and, I might add, he left memories that will not die.

It is my privilege to be able to record some of Billy's thoughts about his life, and I love the title that he suggested, *The Winning Edge.* I have enjoyed writing some of his thoughts, as well as interviewing his children, former players, and coaches. I want to thank you, Coach Henderson, for all the lives you have enriched, including mine, and for all the great memories and stories that are too numerous to tell. I shall treasure always the meetings with you at the Holiday Inn in Athens and at your home, not to mention the many phone calls that we had during this time.

Also, I thank you, Coach, for that wonderful Christian witness that you shared of your loving mother, Jewell, making all those sacrifices in order that you might play sports. I appreciate the mentor that you have become over the years to all your players as well as others like myself who never had the honor of being on one of your teams but learned to love you for the kind, loving human being that you are. I know that your children thank you for the wonderful role model that you have provided for them. God bless you and your family.

***—Aubrey Hammack, M.Ed***
Macon, Georgia

CHAPTER ONE

# TALENT AND DESIRE

*One of the greatest talents of all is the talent to recognize and to develop talent in others.*

*—Frank Tyger, Editorial Cartoonist*

Wally Butts, Billy Henderson, and Jim Whatley after Billy signed with the Macon Peaches

Most would agree that, in order to achieve or to be good at anything, there must be some talent and probably lots of desire, or passion. Innate ability is wonderful and certainly makes achievement easier, but many who have had no outstanding abilities have done great things, simply because they wanted to so badly. This is certainly true in sports.

Some people are destined for greatness in life. It might be in politics, education, medicine, law, science, or writing. Billy Henderson was destined to be a gifted athlete and coach—knowing at an early age that he wanted to be both. While a lad, he excelled in football, baseball, basketball, and track, being blessed with quickness and determination. He had a personality that people were attracted to as well, charisma. In addition he had that million dollar smile, jet black hair, and good looks to go with it. He had something more, however—a burning desire to succeed. Some believe heredity plays a role in this; others feel it is shaped by environmental influences, such as education, financial privilege, and family life. Regardless of how and why it happened, Billy Henderson had that something special that launched him from mere mediocrity to excellence, not just as an outstanding athlete and coach, but also as a parent, relative, and friend who was and is a kind, loving, caring human being. Those who cross his path come out the better for it.

Henderson's talent led him to many interesting experiences, from playing little league baseball in Macon, GA to making all-state baseball from Lanier High School, to playing baseball and football at University of Georgia. During high school, in 1945, Henderson was selected to represent the state of Georgia, in the All American Boys Baseball game. He went to play at the Polo Grounds in New York, with Babe Ruth as his coach for the East. He remembers thinking he had a vision of Babe Ruth as a nice man, a "Boy Scout" idol, if you will. However, Ty Cobb was the coach for the West, and Henderson's perception was that Cobb was "mean, vicious, arrogant, obnoxious." However, he came to see things differently during his short time in New York. During a banquet, Henderson had quite a conversation with a well-dressed gentleman—the man seemed to take an interest in him because he, too, was from Georgia. He didn't know until later that he had spoken with Ty Cobb that evening, but came away impressed by Cobb's manners and articulate speech. Interestingly, the opposite seemed to be true of Babe Ruth. He remembers that Ruth was particularly rude and demeaning when Henderson made a physical error—he threw the ball over someone's head. Ruth yelled from the dugout, cursing, that he needed another catcher. Henderson vividly recalls tears running down his face as he took off the shin guards. And he learned a lesson he would carry through all of his coaching—"Never yell at a young player who makes a physical error—a fumble, an overthrow."

In high school football, too, Henderson was incredibly talented. He remembers seeing Clint Castleberry, of Boys High in Atlanta, play football when Henderson himself was in ninth grade. Castleberry would go on to play for Georgia Tech, and was third in line for the Heisman Trophy as a freshman. However, Castleberry was called up for duty in the Army Air Corps in 1943, and unfortunately, his plane disappeared in 1944 off the coast of Liberia, and was never found. His legend lives on at Georgia Tech, his jersey being the only number ever retired there. To further showcase Henderson's talent, he would go on to break Castleberry's high school scoring record in his senior year at Lanier High School. This might not have happened, however, if his coaches hadn't helped him realize his talent. They understood the importance of the record, and kept him in a game he would otherwise have been taken out of, as Lanier was already in the lead.

When he started at Georgia, he beat out the captain of the baseball team, a senior, for the position of starting catcher. While there, he was three-time MVP for baseball, as well as three-time all-SEC player. In fact,

Henderson still holds UGA's career record in stolen bases—91 total for the years 1947–1950. However, when Coach Wally Butts, his football coach, watched him playing catcher, he told him to change positions because he didn't want one of his running backs in such a dangerous position. Henderson recalls, "I finished my baseball career at Georgia as an outfielder. It was boring. It really was." In his senior year at Georgia, Henderson was drafted as a catcher by the Chicago Cubs, further illustrating the depth of his talent. In addition to baseball, however, Henderson was an outstanding halfback on the football team, and as kickoff return man, he gained 329 yards in 1947, averaging 26.6 yards per return.

As a coach, Henderson knew that it was important to look for the students who had heart, desire to play the game and do well, "no matter what kind of ability they might have." A great many young men who played for Henderson had both, however. He coached three baseball teams to state championships, at Willingham in 1969, and at Mount de Sales in 1971 and 1972. Henderson remembers the especially talented players from that Willingham championship team—Charles Price, first baseman; Wayne Hart, pitcher and first baseman; Donnie Fussell, second baseman; Andy Durden, third baseman; Alan Redmond, shortstop; Richard Tumlin, left field; Billy Beale, center field; Gary Curtis, right field; Charles Hartness, infield; Charles Thompson, first baseman; Tommy Bell, outfield; Bobby Hasty, third baseman; Bob Brown, outfield; Phil Ladson, outfield; Will Goolsby, outfield; Mark Stevens, catcher; and three left-handed pitchers—Chuck Arnold, Jimmy Clanton, and Doug Furney. Edgar Hatcher was also a coach for that team—he particularly remembers that team, saying, "At every position we had a good player, and our bench was just as good as the starters, so it was a very unusual baseball team." He also remembers the greatest game they had. "The day we won the state baseball championship, which was Willingham's only championship, we won both games in extra innings. That made it very exciting." Hatcher also recalls that he and Henderson shared duties coaching third base every other inning, which was quite an honor because Henderson didn't typically have anyone else do that but himself. Clearly, Henderson felt Hatcher had the talent and passion necessary to handle the coaching duties that he himself typically carried out.

Henderson remembers other players that stood out, like Derrell Parker, "one of the most talented athletes" he ever coached. He recalls several instances in which Parker did well, despite adverse circumstances. In one game, he scored a touchdown despite it being a "losing cause." In another game, he continued playing, again scoring a touchdown, although he was tired and wanted to come out of the game. Willingham went on to win that particular game. Henderson also recalls Carson Hardison, who was similar in running style to Darrell Parker—"an outstanding halfback with a great attitude." Hardison was later killed in Vietnam. "Dwight and Ricky Payne were outstanding people, hard-nosed 105 percenters who gave it everything they had. Mark Bowen was one of those talented athletes who played first base on the baseball team and end on the football squad. He had great hands. Jimmy Clay was outstanding all around. I just can't say enough about his attitude—he was a team person. Jeff Wagner was an outstanding fullback. Buck Carroll was small, but, buddy, he gave it all he had, and he was a winner. Claudie Brown played quarterback after Brad was killed, and he was a good one." Henderson describes Pete Gaines as one of those quiet leaders. "He didn't say a lot, but when he spoke, he did it with action." Tommy Hinson, Henderson says, was "born to be a linebacker...one of the better football players...in my career."

Henderson joined the coaching staff at Mount de Sales in 1970 as head baseball coach and assistant football coach. He quickly made his mark, leading the baseball team to championships for two years running. He was subsequently named National Baseball Coach of the year in 1972—further underscoring his talent as a coach, and providing some well-earned accolades. He particularly remembers Ben Zambiasi, who Henderson called "an animal—he scared folks to death, especially at the high school level." He played on both championship teams.

Another favorite of Henderson's was Fran Tarkenton—he played football and baseball at Athens High School (before the schools were combined to create Clarke Central). His talent was obvious from early on. Henderson says, "He was one of the all time natural leaders...when he was a ninth grader, he was in the huddle telling seniors what to do, and in baseball he was a pitcher. He never lost a game." Tarkenton went on to play for the Minnesota Vikings and the New York Giants, and later became a commentator on Monday night football. By the end of his career, he owned every major passing record.

Many remember a very talented young player, John Kasay, who also had a passion for the game. Assistant coach John Barnette remembers football camp at Jekyll Island when Kasay was a freshman. Barnette says that Kasay had two palm trees that he kicked through all the time and talks about how exciting it was. One morning, Kasay came to Barnette, and said, "Coach, can

I work out with the secondary? I'm aware that you take care of kickers." Barnette agreed, and put Kasay in some running drills. In one particular drill, they had snapped the ball and pitched it, and then here comes Kasay—he takes the guy off his feet, and makes a great open field tackle. "Everyone is going nuts…talking about a kicker, a kicker! And, of course, the respect just went through the roof." Barnette continued, "I'm patting him, saying, 'John, that is just great!' and about that time I hear way down the field, 'BARNETTE, BARNETTE YOU'RE FIRED!' I look around like, 'what have I done?'" Coach Henderson runs down the field, much to Barnette's confusion, and he says, "That boy [John Kasay] will be in the NFL playing on Sundays, and he does not need to be there on those types of drills." Of course, Henderson reinstated Barnette within a few minutes. And Coach Henderson was absolutely right—he had recognized very quickly both the talent and desire in John Kasay that would take him to his current position, as kicker for the Carolina Panthers.

Kasay himself says that he "always loved hitting," and admits he wasn't very smart about that. He says now that Coach Henderson realized he had special talent as a kicker, and tried to protect him (which is obvious from Barnette's recollection as well). Kasay remembers in 1982, being halfway through the season playing on the C-team. One of the coaches noticed him and asked Henderson to take a look. The next day, Henderson invited Kasay to come kick with the varsity, and Kasay remembers that from that time forward, he was always allowed opportunities to kick, even though he was still in eighth grade. That following spring, he played in a spring game, and even kicked a couple of field goals. As Kasay continued playing for Henderson throughout high school, he had many fun and memorable experiences. Henderson clearly felt Kasay was very talented, and allowed "a lot of freedom to try whatever field goal I wanted when we crossed the 40 yard line. " He remembers, "My longest field goal was probably 54 yards," though he remembers trying them from 64 and 71 yards.

Henderson also particularly remembers Derek Dooley, who embodies the very definition of talent. He was not only a gifted player, and now coach, but also earned his law degree from the University of Georgia and practiced law for a short time. "He was one of those guys you couldn't find any flaws in—on or off the field—as far as I'm concerned. He is everything a coach would want his player to be. He was a 105 percenter. He led by example. He had a great attitude, and I saw him make one of the greatest runs in the history of football against Lowndes County. We were behind late in the game;

he got a screen pass, probably on the eight-yard line, and he must have run 500 yards across the field. I don't know how many tackles he broke, but he finally collapsed in the end zone, and we won the game. He was recently named the head coach at Tennessee, and of course we were all happy for him. I spoke with him soon after that, and told him that people were asking his mother who she was going to pull for. She said she's already got her orange shirt and cap, and Vince will be a little more subtle with his [red and black]."

CHAPTER TWO

# PREPARATION AND ORGANIZATION

*The will to win is important, but the will to prepare is vital.*
*—Joe Paterno, college football coach*

One of the things that all of Henderson's staff and players remember most about him is that he was very organized and prepared. These lessons have been passed along, as many of these players have gone on to become coaches themselves.

Willingham Coaching Staff, 1964

Coach Henderson had a day-by-day procedure which he felt was critical to success. "Another thing I picked up along the way," Henderson says, "was that kids need to know you have a plan everyday and have a tight schedule. Sometimes I would tear that schedule up and we would start all over. But they knew we HAD a plan and they had confidence in all the coaches. We were blessed on the staff with outstanding people that could help me. The student body was also aware of our goals and ambitions." Henderson's message here is clear—the right people are an important part of preparation as well. Further, he stated that he spent a lot of time teaching the techniques and mechanics of each sport—that he never took these things for granted, that everyone needed to learn, so that when they got to the games, it looked automatic. In addition to the mechanics of each sport, he spent time simulating game situations.

When Henderson went to Clarke Central to take over the reins of a faltering football program, he quickly realized that he needed strategic planning and preparation time. He started meeting with city officials and others at the

Holiday Inn across from the UGA campus every Monday. The back of the restaurant there became known as his office, and is still considered so. Over the years, he met with the mayor and other political figures in Athens, as well as many football players and dignitaries around the state. It was during this early time in Athens that he feels he became a "fund raiser" in addition to being a coach. He remembers times when he'd walk down the streets in Athens, and people would cross to the other side to avoid him, because "they knew what he was after."

Bill Falconer, Clarke Central, Class of 1981 remembers that Coach Henderson "demanded precision in every play, preparation for every game, and leadership both by example and by how you treated fellow teammates. I believe this is why so many Clarke Central football players are succeeding in life, off the football field." Falconer is now coaching in the Northside Youth Organization (NYO) in the Atlanta area.

Another Clarke Central graduate, Ethan Armentrout, recalls that the importance of preparation was instilled throughout Coach Henderson's teaching and coaching. In remembering a championship game, he said, "I discovered that with the proper preparation in life, your goals ARE attainable...no matter how large they may have seemed only a few months earlier."

C H A P T E R   T H R E E

# HARD WORK AND PHYSICAL TRAINING

*If you train hard, you'll not only BE hard, you'll be hard to beat.*

*—Herschel Walker, college and professional football player*

Clarke Central's First Football Camp, 1973

An important part of preparation for Henderson was hard work and physical training. Henderson always said about high school players, "You cannot determine…the talent, you take what you get, and go with it." As a result, he seriously valued the importance of hard work—he and his coaching staff emphasized that no one would outwork his teams. He said, "In the fourth quarter, they [his team] would be in better condition than their opponent. All we ask is 105%." James Holland remembers, "As great a man as he is, he was legendary for being tough. His practices were ruthless. There were no water breaks in those days—we were given hands full of salt tablets to take after practice, as Gatorade hadn't been invented. It was very tough."

Jimmy Hammond remembers specific drills that were tough, like the Board Drill, the Helmet Drill and the Ram Plus Drill, but he also remembers times when "Coach Henderson would send us back to the dressing room after an hour of what we thought had been a hard productive practice, and telling us practice was starting over from the beginning." Bill Falconer remembers something similar—"…winning a game against someone 35 to nothing, Coach announces… 'I didn't like what I saw out there tonight, practice 7 a.m. tomorrow morning.' Laughter was replaced by stunned silence."

A favorite thing that Charles Pledger remembers Coach Henderson saying was, "You're going to hate me now but you will love me later!" Pledger says, "It was so true because during all the extreme workouts, practices, etc. you were, like, 'why am I doing all of this?' but he was teaching us valuable lessons for the real world. Everyone loved Billy because he made you a better person at the end of the day, and most everyone realized that after they had graduated!"

Edgar Hatcher, assistant coach, Willingham baseball, said of Billy, "He never asked anybody to work harder than he did. He had been a great athlete in high school and college (at Georgia) ...always worked hard, and he wanted his coaches [and players] to work just as hard as he did."

Jimmy Hammond told about the perfect example of this. He remembers Coach Henderson running fifty-yard wind sprints on a hot day because he didn't want to ask his players to do anything he hadn't done himself. Another player remembers this same level of determination and hard work, more than fifteen years later. "I remember running the "mile" around that hard asphalt track day after day," recalls Jim Bob Harris. Coach ran them with us. He got the "dry heaves" almost every time! But he was leading by example, showing us, that with a strong mind, you could make your body do more than you thought it could."

When Willingham won the state baseball championship in 1969, Henderson recalls, "Both teams played their hearts out, but I feel our boys worked hard, and deserved it." On June 11, 1969, Willingham played two games against Therrell High School at Luther Williams Field in Macon. The first game was played during the day, with the second being in the evening, with the field lights on. Despite the heat, and exertion of two games (both with extra innings), the boys played hard the entire time. In both games, Wayne Hart delivered good relief pitching, keeping the games tied. In the second game, in the twelfth inning, Hart hit a single, followed by a hit from Redmond, and then another by Jimmy Clanton. The Willingham Rams won the game 2-1, for their first state championship ever.

Coach Henderson's daughter Chris remembers the year that Clarke Central beat Valdosta for the state championship, 1977. It was a very bitter-sweet time because one of their players, Barry Malcolm, had gotten struck by lightning and killed just before the start of school that year. She stated, "I just remember standing in the end zone where the pines are, just praying,

'Please just let us have this victory." The city needed it. This was the first time that Clarke Central had ever known this, and so I just remember when the kick [by Valdosta] got bobbled, and it didn't work. I was just thrilled...I remember going up to my dad and just giving him the biggest hug. It was the culmination of all the hard work everyone put forth."

On a personal level, his children remember their dad as a very hard worker, who was also passionate about what he did. His daughter Fran remembers him as a "wonderful provider for our family, which allowed our mom to stay home." He always made sure they were provided for, and never went without. At times, this meant that he worked a second job at a bowling alley or mini-mart. His daughter Fran remembers that part of his hard work was to make breakfast for all of his children before school each day—eggs, bacon and toast. "He was quite a cook," she said. Additionally, he taught them each the importance of hard work, as they all had jobs and responsibilities inside the home.

Some of the hardest work expected of the players was in the area of physical training. In his youth, Billy Henderson was surrounded by coaches from Lanier High School in Macon, Georgia, who were prime examples of what all coaches should be. Those coaches were H.P. Bell, Cotton Harrison, Lem Clark, and John Stooge Davis. The latter, Coach Davis, was light-years ahead of his time with regards to physical training for his athletes. He lifted weights himself, and ran regularly, as well as having his students do the same. Henderson said, "That physical fitness influenced my life and later my students." Weight conditioning was one of the biggest influences that the coaching staff at Lanier had on him, and Henderson maintains that this is one of the "winning edges," that has contributed to his very successful personal athleticism and coaching career.

Again, when Henderson coached at University of South Carolina, under Warren Geise, they established a weight training program (and again, ahead of their time). It started simply by positioning weights outside the dressing room, and after practice, as players came off the field, they would stop and lift weights.

When Henderson went back to Macon in 1958 to start at a new school, Willingham High School, one of his first priorities was to establish a weight room—he remembers feeling like that was a "winning edge," even though their record the first year was 0-7-3. One of his coaching staff, Jessie Duckworth, had been a fellow player at Lanier High School, and shared the same enthusiasm for weight training. As a result, Duckworth headed up the first weight training program.

While at Willingham, a Marine physical fitness test was developed and disseminated to the public. Coach Henderson had it given to the entire student body, and people liked to say that Willingham High School had the most physically fit student body in the world. Coach Henderson was particularly pleased though, that this was allowed to happen for the entire student body, and not just the athletes. He remarked, "If I've done anything right in teaching and coaching, it was [to do] for the whole student body, not just the team...to carry it over in life."

And yet again, when Coach Henderson went to Athens to coach at Clarke Central, John Barnette recalls that the weight room had been turned into a junk room. Barnette had attended there and graduated before Henderson came. One of Henderson's priorities was to seek out the school superintendent, Dr. Charles McDaniel, and tell him what Clarke Central needed to get the program started. At that time, Dr. McDaniel politely told Coach Henderson, "We appreciate your insight, but you may want to find other employment, because this is what we have [available]." Of course, they developed a fantastic weight training program.

One of the fondest memories many players and coaches have of Coach Henderson is the time they spent in football training camps at Jekyll Island each summer. However, their memories are not related so much to being at the beach, as they are about the hard work and physical training they completed. There was no real time for horsing around or vacation; Jekyll was for hard work and training the entire week.

During the football camps, players had three practices a day, and it was "non-stop," according to Henderson. It was a tough experience, with the goal being to get the young players ready for football season. This same tough approach was used in all practices. Billy Beale remembers that pass protection was done live, and if a lineman missed a block, he played quarterback the next play—in order to teach him how it felt. He too, remembers the legendary football camps at Jekyll, saying, "It's amazing that things I hated at the time are fond memories now."

Approximately five years ago, Coach Henderson was at a book signing with Ed Grisamore, and a young man by the name of Brian Ward came up to have his book signed. Coach said, "He was dressed in his Marine Corps uniform and looked sharp as a tack. I signed it, and he walked away and came back and gave me a bronze medallion symbolic of superiority in physical fitness. Brian said he wanted Coach to have it "because you helped me get it." Coach responded, "How?" Brian then said "Paris Island was a piece of cake compared to Jekyll Island."

Ethan Armentrout, Clarke Central graduate, recalls that while they called training camp "Jek-Hell" Island, in reality, it was a "rite of passage. It was spiritual. It created the bonds that you read about or see on movies. It made men out of boys." He particularly remembers that before he attended camp for the first time, he was "terrified" of heights. But after attending his first camp at Jekyll, he felt he became "fearless to the point he didn't recognize himself." He had grown up. Jim Bob Harris, Clarke Central graduate and player under Bear Bryant, remembers, "It was hot and it was hard, but we had a good time, and really jelled together as a team."

Henderson has always applied these physical fitness expectations to himself, as well as to his teams. Over the years, he has had a personal routine of swimming and playing handball. He has continued that tradition in each place he has lived. In Macon, while at Mount de Sales Academy, he would take a lunch break and walk to the Y to play handball. He remembers that, one day, an acquaintance stopped and asked what was in his briefcase, so he showed him. It was a pair of shorts, a tee shirt, and a jock strap. He has played handball with such fierce competitors as Tommy Hewlett (who he remembers as a tremendous athlete), Bob Berlin, Hubert Howell, and others. Later, in Athens, he developed the habit of swimming everyday at the YMCA.

CHAPTER FOUR

# DISCIPLINE AND HIGH EXPECTATIONS

*Good, better, best. Never let it rest. Till your good is better and your better is best.*

*—Tim Duncan, professional basketball player, San Antonio Spurs*

Mount de Sales State Championship Baseball Team, 1971

Strong discipline (both self-discipline and teaching it to others) and high expectations are important pieces of having the winning edge, in Henderson's viewpoint. Billy Beale, player for Henderson at Willingham, and later a coach himself, remembers this well. He says, "I was about six or seven when Dad took a job at Willingham, so my memories of Henderson start young. My early memories…him and dad letting me grow up on the sidelines of football games and at…practice. As for playing for Coach Henderson, I remember the discipline, the repetition to get things done right. As a quarterback, I remember running perfect plays seemingly forever with all of the coaches looking for a reason to send us back [to do it again.]" Beale also particularly remembers playing baseball for Coach Henderson. It was only one season, but it was a season to remember. "The things you remember," Beale recalls, "are the fundamentals. Everybody could bunt, everybody could run the bases, and everybody played defense. I believe we were in better shape than the track team, and it paid off in the state championship series." Even after winning the games in such heat and extra innings, the coaches asked the players if they wanted to run bases late that night.

The importance of discipline began to be instilled by Henderson even in the little leaguers with whom he worked. Gary White, a member of the Mount de Sales championship baseball teams, played Little League under Henderson first, remembering that even then, if players missed practice, they were given extra running duties the next time. Later on, at MDS, if players didn't pay attention (like White on one occasion), they were made to drop what they were doing, and run the bases.

Bobby Bryant, Willingham High School Class of 1963, remembers Coach Henderson as a "great teacher, not only on football and baseball, but also on character and honor and how to live our lives to become better people." One way in which he taught this was through discipline. Bryant remembers a football practice his junior year, in which he defied Henderson's instructions to run some punishment drills for poor practice. He says, "I think Coach was probably dumbfounded by my insubordinance, because I was normally a compliant person…respectful of authority. Coach did not blow up or yell or scream. He simply told me I could turn my equipment in, which I did. Later that year, he allowed me to come join the baseball team." Bryant states it was a learning experience for him, but the lessons didn't end there. He says now, "I know he had more to do with my getting a football scholarship to South Carolina than I will ever know. Thanks to Coach Henderson, I learned that if you want something bad enough, "It can be done!" Bryant went on to play for the NFL, with the Minnesota Vikings, 1968–1980. However, Coach Henderson says he also learned a lesson from that situation—never to give an ultimatum to a player, especially when you are angry.

He, the coaches, and the players have many memories of those times at Jekyll. Some of the memories revolve around players who thought Jekyll would be more of a vacation…and were quite surprised to find that Coach Henderson was just as tough at Jekyll as he was at home. Several remember the mid-1980s, and a year in which Derek Dooley (now head coach at University of Tennessee), David Perno (head baseball coach at UGA), Randy Williams, and some others had that very idea. The cheerleaders decided to visit camp at the end of the week, and the boys were, of course, happy to see them. They planned to have a camp celebration with the girls on the last night, and didn't think the coaching staff knew. Randy Williams stated that he was not feeling well, so he volunteered to keep watch for any signs of being caught. He saw some coaches roaming around and felt there might be trouble. He snuck out, went to the meeting point, and found everyone celebrating. Williams explained that he was worried, but another teammate said, "Look, we've made it through camp, we're going home tomorrow, there is no practice, and if we are caught...what are they going to do until we get home? Get in the car and come with us." Williams decided to join in the celebration and stayed with his teammates. They got back to their rooms with no confrontations and assumed everything was fine.

Henderson stated, "They didn't think I knew, but one of my coaches was waiting for them, recorded their names, but didn't say a word (not that night anyway)." The next day, they were practicing "light" as it was almost time to return home. The players were in shorts. All appeared fine until about 11 a.m., when Coach pulled the players together, and called out the names of the boys who had snuck out. He also said, "If anybody else went with them, you better tell me now or you are going to die." Those particular boys had to put on full gear, and then were run through the 'hat drill,' in which players run around staggered helmets, and then sprint around the last one. Coach told them, "Don't let up until you pass me, 'cause I'm gonna kill y'all." Williams remembers that Coach then said, "Get running or go home!" Sure enough, toward the end, they were dragging. By then, the squad knew they had been punished enough. Williams said he doesn't even remember how many sets they ran, but he does remember sleeping on the bus ride home. Coach said, "I never penalized them for a game because that's cutting your nose off to spite your face. I then told them I was proud of them, and all is forgotten." Dooley remembers that this was the maddest he ever saw Coach Henderson. "We probably ran the longest hats in the history of Clarke Central...he wore us out."

John Kasay, who has gone on to play professional football, had a similar story to Derek Dooley's. Coach Henderson's daughter Carol remembers that particular summer well. She said that players would often try to sneak out between meetings and meals, and go out to the beach. On one particular evening, they received a knock on their hotel room door, from the grandparents of a girl also visiting Jekyll. They said they couldn't find their granddaughter, who was eighteen, and they suspected she was with John Kasay (who they didn't know). At that time, Kasay was about fifteen, and Carol recalled that her mother, Fosky Henderson, suddenly got very worried about John, being with an eighteen-year-old! However, it wasn't long until Kasay got word that everyone was looking for him, and he came to the Henderson's hotel room, with what Carol described as a "very meek knock."

Kasay himself remembers more about the toughness of the camps at Jekyll. He said everyone had an expectation of going to the beach...thinking how nice that was going to be, but in the end, no one even noticed the water. They were kept busy with two-a-day workouts, meetings, sleeping, and eating, with very little free time. When they arrived for Kasay's first time at Jekyll, he recalls, "We didn't get to our rooms as quickly as Henderson expected us to, and there were probably 120 of us, including C-team, junior varsity, and varsity. So our punishment was a drill he called 'the hat,' and I didn't know what hats were until that moment...I knew when I left Jekyll EXACTLY what they were. The hats are put about five yards apart, and spread out on a distance between the hashes, so it's probably a twenty-yard width and a five-yard depth, and you just run around each of those in a zig zag way. You do the math—with 120 helmets, and we probably were running 500 to 600 yards." However, Kasay also remembers how the players bonded as a team through camp, and he feels if he were a high school coach, he would do something similar to the Jekyll experience.

The hat drill wasn't new when John Kasay experienced it—Claudie Brown remembers that drill from when he attended Jekyll Island Camps in the early 1960s. "Jekyll Island was no fun!" He remembers three-a day-workouts, and "if you broke curfew (not in room by 9:00 pm), you were in serious trouble. And he [Coach] always used hat drills as punishment." Claudie played quarterback for the Willingham Rams after Brad Henderson was killed in a tragic car accident in 1964.

Willie Green remembers the Jekyll Island experiences as something they took pride in, because others weren't doing this. "Coach Henderson was way ahead of his time—we didn't realize then that practice on the sand made us faster, it made us stronger." He sees more people training in this way now, because they realize the strength you build by running and training on the sand.

Randy Williams also remembers another kind of situation when a player didn't follow instructions. He says that the 1985 team had two great tailbacks—Kenny Brown and Richard Jewell. The week of the state championship game, Williams recalls that Jewell didn't agree with some of the substitution plans for the game. It seems that he irritated Coach Henderson during practice, and Coach finally told him to "Get off the field." Williams said they weren't sure they would have Jewell back for the state championship, which made them nervous. "As teammates, we were aware he would have to follow "Billy's rules," and we also knew that you better not even TRY to tell Coach what to do, but we also really believed we needed Richard." This created extreme stress on the team. They decided to "kidnap" Richard Jewell, which they did after eating dinner together one night. Instead of taking Richard home, they drove to Coach Henderson's house. When they got there, they told Jewell they had been through too much together, and he needed to go APOLOGIZE to Coach. They kicked him out of the jeep into the cold. Williams remembers that they provided a little verbal encouragement and then drove off. None of them knows what was said between Jewell and Coach Henderson, or how Jewell got home, but Jewell was at practice the next day, and ended up scoring the game-breaking touchdown for the 1985 State Championship. Jewell went on to play football at Georgia Southern with a scholarship, later joined the Navy, and is recently retired from the Pentagon.

Derek Dooley, now head football coach at the University of Tennessee, said these high expectations underlie one of his most vivid memories of Coach Henderson. "In my senior year, we were playing Cedar Shoals, our cross town rival. For years, Cedar [Shoals] and Clarke [Central] played in the same stadium, AT Clarke Central. So even though we might have been "visitor" in our own stadium, it always felt like we had home field advantage. Before my senior year, Cedar had built their own stadium on campus, so that was going to be their year to come and put it to us. But we finally had to go to their place to East Athens, so it was a big game, to say the least. We went out, and we were beating them seventeen to nothing at half time. We felt like we were doing pretty good, but Coach Henderson was just on fire. I mean, he wanted to beat them so bad. We didn't even go into our locker room. At half time, he pulled us right off the field, and we sat and did 'bull in the ring' the entire half. We just started hitting each other. 'Bull in the ring' is an old school, physical hitting drill. Then he told us we were going to take the opening kickoff, and we were only going to run two plays the rest of the game—42 or 43 to the right or left or 46, which is an off-tackle power play, to the right or left. We got the ball on the fifteen-yard line, and I'm telling you, I think we went about fifteen plays total in the third quarter. He [Coach] was yelling the play from the sideline and TELLING Cedar Shoals what we were running, saying we're going to tell them what play we're doing, and they're not going to stop it, and WE SCORED. It was unbelievable how he can just WILL things to happen. We ran it every snap, and we just grinded it, and just kept hitting them."

Another expectation that Coach Henderson had was regarding how his coaching staff conducted themselves in public. His son-in-law, Steve Brooks, recalls that when he joined the coaching staff at Clarke Central the first year, he had a favorite restaurant. He would just go there to eat (best steak and cheese sandwich anywhere!), hang out, and play shuffleboard, because hardly anyone else would go there. However, Coach Henderson called him in one day and said, "If I ever catch you in there again, I'll dismiss you from the staff. If you are going to be a coach, a teacher, you can't go to places like that." He told Brooks that he had to be above reproach, that he had to be a good example of what a coach and teacher was. Coach Henderson didn't drink or go to bars, and he didn't want his staff to do that either. And Brooks says now, "Henderson didn't just talk it, he lived it. Those lessons have stuck with me. I want to be that kind of coach and father." Brooks now coaches at Oconee High School.

Henderson also had high expectations of himself. His friend Bob Berlin (a lawyer and mediator) shared a funny story about this. They often played handball together, and on one particular day, Bob heard Billy muttering as he approached the handball court. "As he got closer, I could hear him say, 'I'm going to whip his butt! I'm going to whip his butt! I'm going to whip his butt!' Sure enough, he was psyching himself up to play me—Bob "Who Hates To Lose" Berlin. Anyone who knows Billy knows that he too, refuses to lose. After a brief warm-up (I believe Billy's mouth was still running about how badly he was going to beat me), we played 'the man's game.' Billy banged into all four walls throughout the hour. I found myself constantly getting out of his way to avoid a collision as he chased the ball. To my surprise, he went after EVERY ball. Whew! What a stroke of luck I was not injured." All three games that day resulted in scores of 21-20, with Billy Henderson winning two of the three games. Berlin states, "In fact, upon winning the third game, he let out a victory scream as loud as a wounded elephant. I ducked, not knowing what I was hearing and what would come next!" For the next three weeks, Henderson reminded Berlin everyday of who won. Berlin said jokingly, "Billy must have thought I had Alzheimer's disease!"

CHAPTER FIVE

# TEAMWORK AND TEAM BUILDING

*Commitment to the team—there's no such thing as in-between. There's either in or out.*

*—Pat Riley, NBA basketball coach*

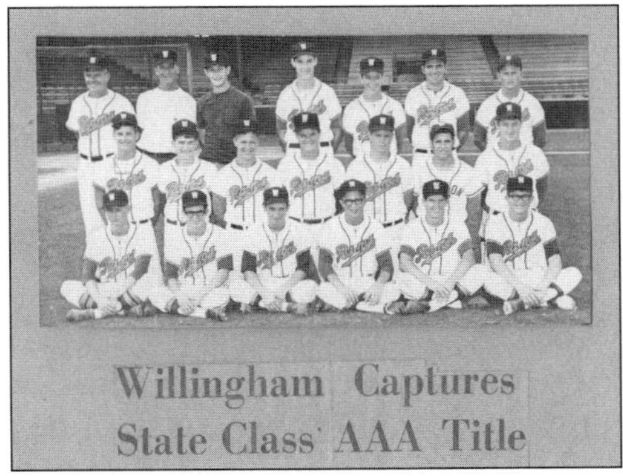

Willingham State Championship Baseball Team, 1969

Coach Henderson was ahead of his time in terms of conducting "team building exercises." When he was in Athens, he petitioned the mayor to allow his students to help clean up the city. After storms had come through, and various debris was around town, they would have the students and parents meet at school, ride out in city trucks, and pick up trash from the storm. Each student was paid minimum wage, and each would donate the money to the boosters' club. Henderson felt that, "the beautiful part…is that those kids saw what labor was…" He was always right beside the students and parents, doing his part as well, and leading by example. He felt that this type of teamwork, doing things together outside of the required practices and games, was one of the winning edges. Willie Green remembers this experience well, saying, "You have to understand how we got to go to Jekyll Island. Coach Henderson made us realize that nothing in life is going to be given to you. You've got to work for it. What we did in order to go—one Saturday out of the year we had to walk and clean up the entire city of Athens. We would pick up trash the whole day, and we LOOKED FORWARD to doing that. That was a way for us to raise money to go to Jekyll. It taught us work ethic. It taught us nothing is given to you. You have to work for what you want in life. It instilled a habit in us that nobody is going to do anything for you, unless you do it for yourself."

This type of team building was fostered throughout Henderson's career. When the teams traveled to Jekyll each year for training, they did everything together. They practiced, worked out, played, ate, and slept together. Henderson felt that this kind of togetherness "brings you together as a family." Willie Green said, "The Jekyll Island experience was to us like a rite of passage into a family. It was something we took pride in. It was just being with the fellows, being there with your teammates where we were sharing—black and white, rich or poor. Typically you don't see that. I think it brought us closer together. All of us were one family. I know David Perno, Chris Morocco, Greg Reeves, Doug Davenport, Jerry Reid, Jerry Harris. Derek Dooley. We still communicate to this day, and every time, we talk about Jekyll Island." However, another part of feeling like family, Green felt, was Fosky, Coach's wife. "Fosky was Coach Henderson's rock, and she was like a mother to us. You can't forget her." Jim Bob Harris remembers her as well, saying, "Fosky Henderson. Now there was a smile and sparkle all in one. She loved us all."

Even players who did not play much learned they were important members of the team. Ethan Armentrout recalled that, while he did not play much in 1992 (his sophomore year), that even when he didn't play in the games, he was still part of the team; he still helped prepare his teammates for their contributions to the games. "This attitude translated into the value of working together as a team," Armentrout said, "You know you're doing it right when it has more of a family feeling to it. We would fight in practice, but there was no denying the bond that was formed between all of us. Those bonds still exist today—seeing anyone is like running into a cousin; homecoming is more like a family reunion."

Sometimes the lessons of teamwork didn't feel so great at the time—Doug Furney recalls playing baseball for Coach Henderson at Willingham in 1969: "We had a lot of good players on that team but not any great players. Coach Henderson and Coach Hatcher did a great job of utilizing the talent we had. We relied on good pitching, great defense and timely hitting from a lot of different players. We had a lot of close games, and it seemed that Coach Henderson always made the right move at the right time to win the game. I remember in the quarter-finals of the state against Moultrie, we had won the first game at their park in extra innings and lost the second game the next day at Luther Williams Field in Macon. This set up the rubber game, and I was the starting pitcher. It was about the fifth inning and the score was tied 0-0. I don't think I had given up a hit to that point. They got two runners on base, and Coach Henderson came out to the mound and took me out and brought in Chuck Arnold. I was pretty mad at the time. We went on to win the game and, after it was over, Coach Henderson looked at me and said, 'You probably hate me right now, but I did what was best for the team.' I realized then that he was right. He had to make a lot of decisions that year, but *he always did what was best for the team."* Furney is currently the director of Lake Tobesofkee in Macon.

Even in very serious matters, Henderson emphasized the importance of being a team. Bill Falconer, Clarke Central, Class of 1981, recalls a very trying time. "On my first day of school as a sophomore, a large, racially charged brawl broke out in the hallways, requiring police to roam the halls for months. Coach held a team meeting prior to practice that day. He paced across the room while he spoke, staring at us with a seriousness I had never seen before, even during a game. He demanded that no football player would ever be involved in that 'crap,' as we were NOT black and white, we were brothers and teammates. When I walked to the coin toss as captain two years later, holding hands with two black teammates, I remember how proud I was to be associated with Clarke Central football and my teammates." Willie Green remembers, "Playing at Clarke Central was like being part of a family where race didn't matter, economic status didn't matter. Nothing mattered if you were on that team. You were part of a family. To show you how extensive that family was—if the community saw a football or basketball player walking around town, the community would say, 'Get your butt back to that school! You've got a future.' That's what you saw at Clarke Central—you saw a family." Jim Bob Harris had this same feeling—"I remember coming into CCHS as a ninth-grader with my guys from the Y-days, and blending almost immediately with a group of guys from another part of town. Coach Henderson didn't care what color we were or where we grew up. His leadership in that regard allowed, not only those of us on the football team, but everybody at the school to establish friendships that may never have happened."

Another Clarke Central player, and later, coach, Randy Williams, felt it was an absolute dream and honor to play for Coach Henderson. He said, "Coach Henderson not only led the team, he was the heartbeat of our community and father figure to thousands of young people." He had that infamous "it" factor, according to Williams—"He brought all walks of life to one common purpose, for the good of our community. Rich, poor, black, white, male, or female...Coach Henderson provided the leadership of one heartbeat for personal development and athletic excellence." In fact, Williams says he didn't understand what political differences were until he left high school, due to Coach Henderson's ability to have everyone working together as a family, toward common goals.

With the coaches, too, there was teamwork and team building. Steve Brooks, Henderson's son-in-law, recalls that at Clarke Central, all the coaches were friends. They went on vacation together, played golf together, taught together, and ate Sunday meals together. In fact, another assistant coach, John Barnette, lived with the Brooks family for approximately six months, which further strengthened their bond. Henderson says, "I tried to help create an environment that I personally had at Lanier where all the coaches helped each other. We saw that in football at Willingham. When football season was over, they put the gear up, and then we had basketball and, in the spring, track, baseball, and other spring sports."

CHAPTER SIX

# PARENT AND COMMUNITY INVOLVEMENT

*The common denominator is that we want to make the world a better place…and we do it through sports.*
*—Lyn St. James, Indy Rookie of the Year*

Coach Henderson always felt like the parents were a part of the Winning Edge. Fred Johnson, principal at Willingham, remembers very well how Henderson worked to get many parents involved, "The parents and the program steadily increased under Henderson's guidance." Coach always said that parents want the very best for their children, and so the first thing they did every August was to have a meeting in the weight room with all the parents. They'd meet the coaches, who would go over the expectations. The first expectation was that the classroom had priority over everything—it was number one. Then they would talk about practice sessions and football camp. All players were expected to attend the camp at Jekyll Island, perform well and conduct themselves appropriately. This meant following the rules—Coach Henderson's rules—to a T.

Billy throwing out the first pitch for a Little League game

Beyond the players and coaching staff, Billy Henderson has always worked hard to garner community support and civic pride. He always felt that communities were paramount to having successful football programs. He says, "We did everything we could to get that involvement. We would go to civic clubs to promote what we were trying to do, we went to every elementary school in Macon, we had film clips of…what athletics can do for a child…and we had great success at Willingham with the community and the parents." Henderson's dear friend Jessie Duckworth always said, "You could have the greatest products in the world, and if people don't know about it, they won't respond." So they always felt that the involvement of the community is essential—an important part of the team. Coach Henderson specifically remembers his first years at Willingham, when he was recruiting kids and recruiting community support for fundraising. They had recruited 175 kids, and the athletic director, Selby Buck, thought there was no way they could get uniforms for all of them. Henderson said, "We will find a way to get them because if they come out [for the team], every one of them is going to get a uniform. And they did."

One of the ways Henderson involved the community in Macon was through his creation, McWill Night, which began at Willingham. Fred Johnson, principal at Willingham during Henderson's time there, remembers that finances were always an issue for athletics at Willingham, which inspired Coach Henderson to create McWill Night. He describes this as a physical education extravaganza demonstration. Through this, a great deal of money was raised for all athletic programs. Henderson's daughter Fran remembers, "It was a magical night—everyone came together as groups…with different athletic abilities." The theme song for the event was, "The Impossible Dream," Henderson's favorite song. "He truly believes nothing is impossible," said Fran. "He had a gift of bringing everyone together to strive for the same purpose." A memorable night was when Jimmy Carter and Lester Maddox were both there demonstrating physical fitness, with Carter in his running shorts and Maddox riding his bicycle backwards.

Fred Johnson recalls that, "Billy is one of the most enthusiastic people that I have ever known. He's a promoter from way back. He promoted athletics, he promoted physical fitness, he promoted the academic side of the school…but for all his ability to promote, he never promoted himself. He didn't want to tell you what a great guy he was. He promoted programs and things that would help other people. That's what I remember about him."

On a more individual note, there were certain people in the community who became incredible supporters of Coach Henderson and his teams. These people, it could be argued, played an important role in the teamwork involved in success—another Winning Edge. One of Willingham's biggest fans was a young man named Johnny Higdon, a former football player there. He was injured at the age of sixteen after falling from a tree. Henderson remembers, "Johnny Higdon was 6 feet tall and considered to be a college prospect. One day he was out in Warner Robins playing with his buddies, had climbed to the top of a tree, and fell out right onto his head. Next thing I know, I was visiting him in the hospital, and he's in a coma." After some time, Higdon came out of the coma, and when he had recovered enough to leave the hospital, the first place he wanted to go was Willingham High School. Henderson said, "I could cry thinking about it, because he loved it [Willingham]. In fact he had blue and white blood. And he became part of us." The coaches alternated picking him up every morning, taking him home in the evenings. "You're talking about the Winning Edge, Johnny Higdon would get on the track with the PE students, and he would do the same thing they were doing. Only he would fall down twenty times getting around the track, and each time he got up, the students would stand up and cheer." Higdon also attended football games regularly, carrying his megaphone. After Henderson moved over to Mount de Sales Academy in Macon, Higdon followed him over and became a fan, cheering for the Cavaliers. This strength of character, enthusiasm and determination are critical elements in teamwork and success of any kind.

Carl "Bulldog" Hudson, Louie Wanniger, Dan Thurston, and Billy Henderson, Lanier High School, 1944

Billy slides in safely in UGA-Ga. Tech game

Jim Bagwell, Austin Eason, and Billy Henderson, UGA Baseball

Billy Henderson—UGA Baseball (Courtesy of Guest Photographers)

Weyman Sellars, Captain Chester Leather, Agnew Peacock,
and Billy Henderson—Athens High School, 1954

Billy Henderson—UGA Football

Wally Butts, Joe Geri, Johnny Rauch, John Tillitski, and Billy Henderson, UGA

Henderson Family, Christmas 1956, Columbia, South Carolina

Brad Henderson, 1956, Greenville, South Carolina

Supt. Mark Smith, Judge Stevens, and Billy, February 1958

Fran, Carol, Chris, Johnny, and Brad Henderson, Macon Zoo

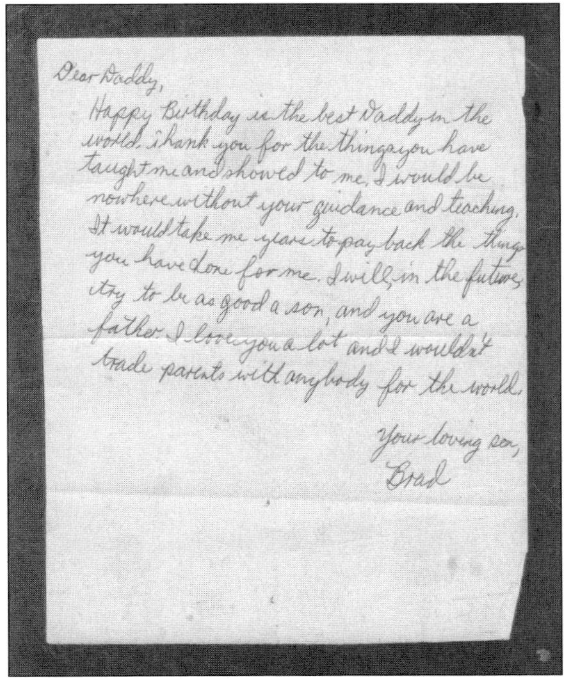

Dear Daddy,

Happy Birthday is the best Daddy in the world. Thank you for the things you have taught me and showed to me. I would be nowhere without your guidance and teaching. It would take me years to pay back the things you have done for me. I will, in the future, try to be as good a son, and you are a father. I love you a lot and I wouldn't trade parents with anybody for the world.

Your loving son,
Brad

Brad's letter to his Dad

Dear Mama,
I didn't get you a
present for Mother's Day,
but I wont you to let you know
that I didn't forget. I
love you a lot and I
wouldn't have any other
mother in the world except
you. I'll try to mind
you as much as I can,
because you are so
nice to me and you do
things for me. I love
you very much.

Love Brad

Brad's letter to his Mom

Brad, Fran, Carol, Johnny, and Chris Henderson, 1961

Clint Tucker in Willingham-Lanier game, Nov. 11, 1960

Terry Colson, Billy Henderson, Claudie Brown, Willingham, 1963

Brad Henderson, Tenth Grade

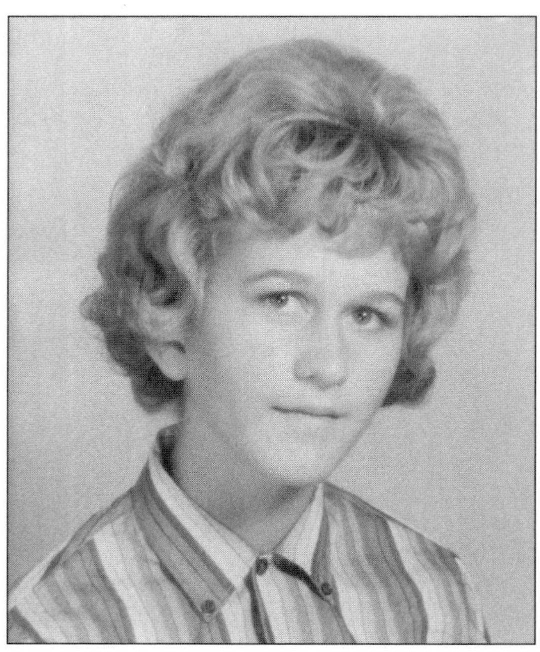

Diane Driggars, Brad's girlfriend,Tenth Grade

Jack Evans handing off to Ralph Alligood, 1964

Fran Henderson with the Willingham-McEvoy Cheerleaders

Carol Henderson with the Willingham-McEvoy Cheerleaders

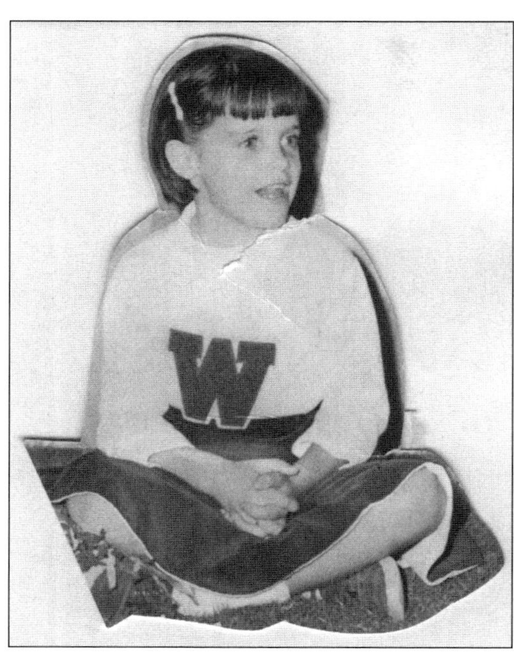

Chris at Willingham, 5 years old

Brad Henderson Memorial Stadium Dedication, Macon, 1964

Billy and Fran, Homecoming Queen, 1969

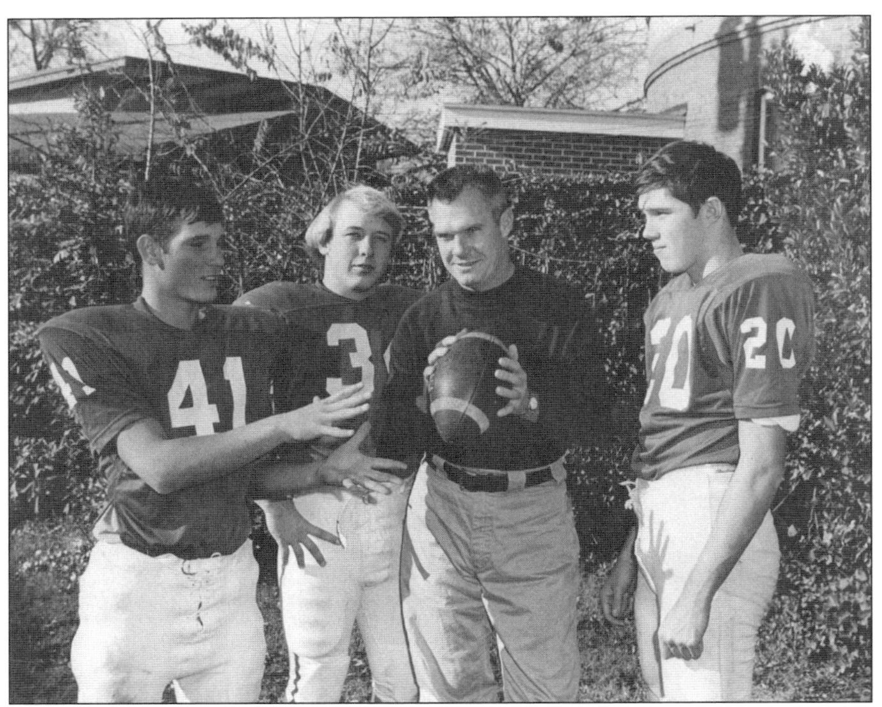

Jimmy King, Tim Jackson, Billy Henderson, and Jimmy Viviani, Mount de Sales

Johnny and Billy, Mount de Sales, 1972

Johnny Henderson, University of Georgia, 1974

Johnny and Billy, 1989

The Macon Telegraph

FRIDAY MORNING, MARCH 23, 1973 PAGE 1B

# Macon Bids Farewell To Billy Henderson

By TOMMY DESSELLE
Telegraph Sports Writer

With his theme song "The mpossible Dream" being layed to open the event, Maconites bade farewell to Coach Billy Henderson and is family Thursday night.

Thursday was "Billy Henerson Day" in Macon and a rowd of 225 people paid tribte to the man who has been oaching in the city since 958.

The Rev. Jimmy Waters as the keynote speaker statg, "We both learned from ach other. Billy taught me ou should always play hard nd play to win."

Sister Mary Fidelis, princial at Mt. de Sales, added, Billy is a man of outstanding aith. He's an excellent coach nd teacher."

Former Maconite Cloyd all, a special assistant to ov. Jimmy Carter, recalled ome of Henderson's feats uring high school. Hall also resented Henderson a plaque om the governor.

George (Squawky) Folsom resented a plapue entitled A Lession in Sportsmanship" Henderson from the Macon andball Association.

Jack Robertson gave Henerson a plaque for his leadrship and service to the comunity, especially with the outh of the city.

A check, showing the appreciation from Henderson's former players and numerous friends was also presented to the coach.

Other speakers included Johnny Higdon, Harley Bowers and Wayne Bevill, who also served as master of ceremonies.

"It's been a privilege to have been involved in these activities," Henderson said. "I'll hold many memories for a long, long time. The last 15 years of my life in Macon have been very rewardi

Henderson, who has ac ed a post at Clarke-Co in Athens, leaves for his job May 1.

Photo by Fred Mattn

*The Rev. Jimmy Waters Bids Farewell To the Hendersons*

L-R., Mrs. Foskey Henderson, Rev. Waters, Coach Billy Henderson

Macon says goodbye to Hendersons, March 23, 1973

Clarke Central Crew Cut picture with Mike Gaines, Todd Clarke,
Jack Langford, Charles Griffiths, Bob McLeod, Mark Ozburn, and Billy, 1975

Jim McGinley and Coach Henderson celebrating 100 wins, Clarke Central

Billy and referee having a conversation, Clarke Central

Derek Dooley, Scott Mitchell, and Billy, Clarke Central, 1984

Billy and Robbie Kamerschen, Clarke Central, 1984

Billy on the sidelines, cheering for his team, Clarke Central

BIlly Henderson, shortly before his retirement, 1995

Last picture day at Clarke Central, 1995

The marker at Billy Henderson Stadium

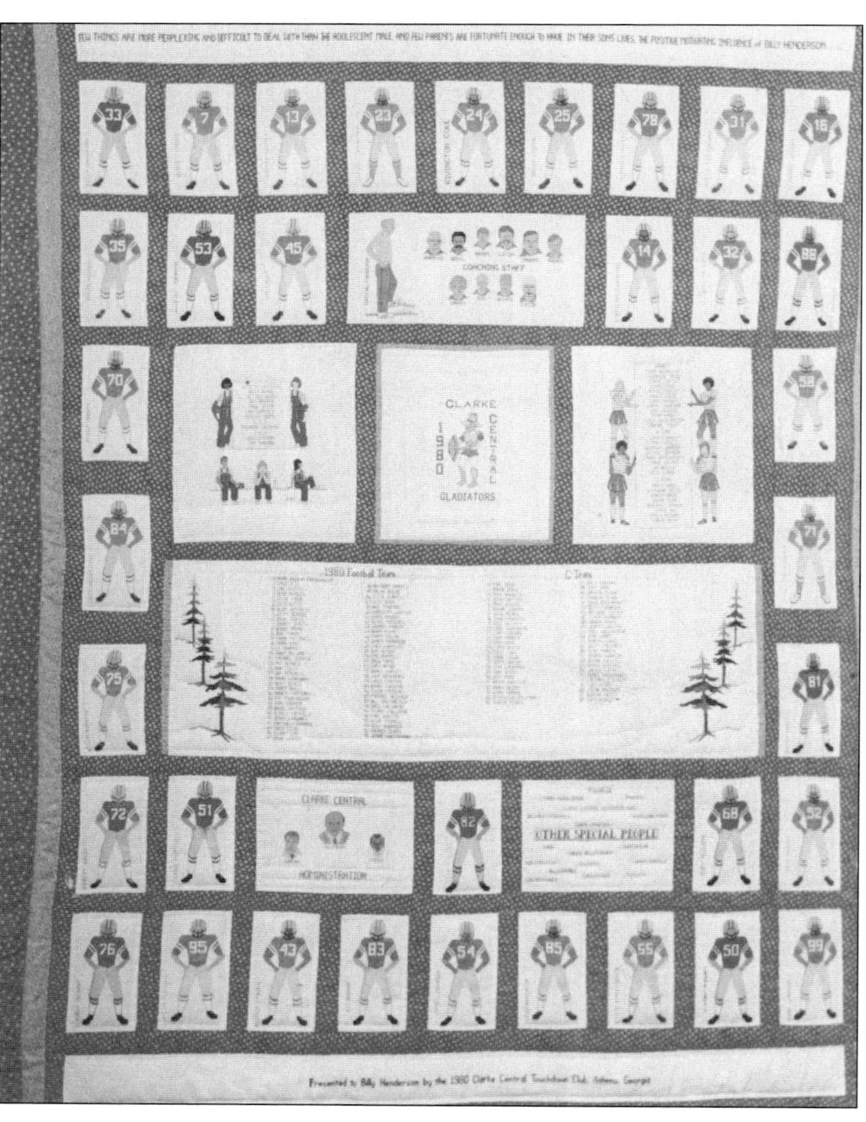


Fosky's Quilt made by the Clarke Central moms

Billy and Fran Tarkenton

Nate Wright and Bobby Bryant, Minessota Vikings

Henderson Family Reunion, 1989

With Highest Regards
To Billy Henderson
A Great Coach, Father
and Friend
Vince Dooley
9-10-93

Billy Henderson and Vince Dooley, 1993

Billy with granddaughter Stefanie Brooks,
Homecoming Queen, 1996

Carol's family—Stefanie, Sarah, Carol, Craig, Steve, 2000

Billy with Gov. Perdue and others, 2004

Henderson Family, 2010

Billy and Fosky's last picture together, 2009

Sarah Brooks, homecoming queen, 2010, with her dad, Steve Brooks

Johnny Henderson and Gary White, Henderson Tribute Event, Macon, 2010

Matthew, Zack, and Chris (Henderson) Watts, Henderson Tribute Event, Macon, 2010

Billy and Jack Evans, Henderson Tribute Event, Macon, 2010

CHAPTER SEVEN

# MOTIVATION

*You can motivate players better with kind words than you can with a whip.*

—*Bud Wilkinson, football player, college football coach, broadcaster*

Coach Henderson has been such a powerful motivator to so many—there are numerous stories, from players of all ages and from all the schools at which he coached.

Billy and John Kasay

Edgar Hatcher: "He knows how to motivate people to do their very best. He cares about people." Billy Beale, player under both Coach Henderson and Coach Hatcher, says he will "always, always, always remember his [Henderson's] ability to motivate young men. He could probably have been a millionaire if he had been a salesman. It's the good fortune of many student athletes in Macon and Athens that working with young people was important to him."

Sometimes, all it took to motivate was talking to a young man who needed to be noticed. Jimmy Hammond met Coach Henderson in 1958, in the parking lot of a Dairy Queen on Houston Avenue in Macon. Jimmy felt that he was already "falling through the cracks," but after talking with Coach Henderson, he played football for him, then went on to play college football, earn a master's degree, and become a teacher and a coach. He attributes his success in large part to Henderson's motivation and guidance.

Another such young man was Bill Falconer at Clarke Central. "As a freshman, I wanted to quickly get Coach Henderson's attention. He mentioned needing his lawn mowed, and I jumped on it. I could not believe he paid me! After I was done, Fosky served me the best sweet tea I had ever had, and Billy spent at least an hour showing me photo after photo of the boys that played for him, each with a brief story. From that day forward, I would have followed Billy over a cliff. And I mowed his lawn every chance I received." When Falconer first began playing in games, he was told by some senior players that he had "better grow up quickly." He must have looked concerned as he came off the field, because Henderson came over and said, "Relax out there. This game will be much easier than practice with Charlie and Mac…if you don't toughen up." Falconer said that was all the motivation he needed! However, Henderson's lessons in motivation for Falconer did not end there. "Coach Henderson is by far the second best male mentor of my forty-seven-year life, next to my father. I draw upon his teachings and philosophies every single day of my life, both personally and professionally, especially when my back is up against the wall. Nothing in my life has been as tough as playing for Coach; he extracted everything out of me and more, due to his supreme ability to motivate one beyond his capabilities. That motivation was driven in many ways: a) his references to the pain of his…son Brad's horrific death—it made you feel lucky to be out there; b) his ability to ensure that the not-so-talented players felt like they were equally important to the success of our team. Everyone respected that and learned to respect each other…; c)we prayed together, enough said; d)workouts and practices that were so demanding that players developed a camaraderie analogous to soldiers at war; e) he cared about us deeply, f)his coaching staff were great guys with great personalities, reflecting Coach's character and beliefs; g) his personality was awesome…; and finally; h) he would play the "Impossible Dream,"…prior to the game in a silent room. It all seems comical now, but it worked!"

Pete Gaines, quarterback for the Willingham Rams in 1962, remembers a particular game in 1962—a cold, wet, November night at the old Porter Stadium. "We were down 6-0 to Lanier. They had quick-kicked to our eighteen. Ten and a half minutes remained in the game, and our offense had been ineffective all night. We were facing a pretty stiff wind and a big mobile defense. The drive consisted of twenty-four plays—all rushing—and four times we converted fourth downs. Our longest run was ten yards. We scored with fifty-three seconds remaining when I sneaked across from the one-half yard line. It was our third consecutive win over Lanier." Gaines commented, "That game was a testimonial to the ability of Coach Henderson to motivate young men when faced with adversity. He remains a tremendous inspiration to so many people—young and old."

Alan Redmond, Willingham High School, Class of 1970, met Coach Henderson in 1965. As Redmond entered the eighth grade, his family moved across the street from the Hendersons. He recalls that Coach Henderson tried to get him to play ball in the eighth grade, though he didn't end up doing that. However, Henderson did talk Redmond into going to the infamous Jekyll football camp the next summer. Redmond believes, "He is the greatest motivator that I have ever been around. His way of motivating me was that, before we left for Jekyll, he put me on the blue team (first team offense). I didn't realize this was his way of getting me excited. Less than an hour into our first practice, I was not on blue, but was back with the B-team, scrimmaging against the varsity. He had me hooked though." Redmond ended up playing four years of football and two years of baseball with Coach Henderson, and was on the 1969 state championship baseball team.

Former Clarke Central player Charles Pledger refers to Billy as the master motivator. He tells this story to illustrate: "My senior year, we were playing a team and winning 28-0 at the half, so we go into the opposing team gym to some bleachers on the second level which overlooked the main gym. As players, we were on cloud nine, since we were winning 28-0. That lasted about two minutes because Billy walked in and threw a large trash container over the second story balcony onto the gym floor below, which quickly got everyone's attention. Then he threatened us with a Saturday 6 a.m. practice (trust me, I went through one my junior year and it was an absolute hell) if we didn't score the opening drive of the second half. I can assure you that no one wanted to practice at 6 a.m. so we took the ball and drove it down and scored. This is just one example of how he took young men, motivated them and made them work together to achieve the same goal." However, Pledger also remembers a different kind of motivation—"Game days: This was special... there was nothing like showing up at Clarke Central on Game days. You knew once you walked into the gym, it was business. There was no joking around, no horse playing once you entered the gym doors. As you prepared to play that night, you could see the intensity building as the game got closer. I still get goose bumps when I hear the

Rocky fight song and remember holding hands in the weight room, waiting on Billy to give us his pre-game speech. *He made everyone feel like they could run through a brick wall.* I had the luxury to play at the University of Georgia, and, I can assure you, that the pre-game rituals were not as intense!"

Coach Henderson believes that a great motivator is an audience—it worked quite well each year at the Jekyll camps to have the players' families come along, if possible. The crowd of parents and siblings watched practices, which "motivated the kids to do better."

# CHAPTER EIGHT

# POSITIVE ATTITUDE, CONFIDENCE, AND ENTHUSIASM

*If you believe in yourself, have dedication and pride, and never quit, you'll be a winner.*

*—Paul "Bear" Bryant, college football coach*

Billy, Gov. Zell Miller, and Randy Williams at Clarke Central Stadium

Coach Henderson believed it was incredibly important to build confidence in each young athlete. "Confidence is developed by putting kids in situations where they can succeed, and when they succeed, comment on it." He did that with young players, and his own children, by teaching them to hit with a bat, using tennis balls, knowing it would be easier to start hitting tennis balls than baseballs. He was fond of saying, "Hitting is 100% mental. You have to go up there knowing you can hit the ball." He also felt it was important to be loose and relaxed. He remembers being taught these things when HE was a child—from coaches such as H.P. Bell, who he said made him feel the baseball was as big as a basketball, and Lem Clark, who was fiery and full of determination. Another way in which Henderson built confidence in his young players was teaching them specific techniques to increase odds of success. Gary White, baseball player for Mount de Sales, remembers that Coach Henderson taught him several techniques regarding pitching, picking off first-base runners, and giving signals to teammates. In fact, White had played under Henderson starting in Little League, at the age of 8 or 9 years. This effort at building confidence in his players had begun at those young ages. White recalls that, in one particular game, he wasn't pitching well, but Coach Henderson had confidence in him, allowed him to finish the game, and they won.

Jimmy Hammond, player at Willingham and later a coach under Henderson, recalls that Henderson taught him early on to "always hold my head up, to look up, not to drop my head down." Larry Evans also remembers these kinds of lessons in confidence. "Billy Henderson was a person that taught young men and women that if you embraced the …small things in life, it would help you with the big picture of success. My favorite was teaching young men and women the importance of looking someone in the eye when he is talking to you or you are speaking to him. He also had the skill of creating a small skill into a confidence builder with letting everyone around know, 'I caught someone doing it right, and let's celebrate it.' I will never forget when I first went out for football, running a drill of one-on-one, that he stopped all of practice to let everyone know Chipper Murphy and myself were doing it like it should be done, to come and watch." Evans felt that the confidence he gained in eighth grade from that experience, he carried throughout high school and life.

Coach Henderson had such a positive attitude, and with it came positive, confident speech. Steve Brooks, Henderson's son-in-law, remembers a particular game in which he felt Henderson just talked them through to victory. Clarke Central was playing Warner Robins, and Brooks said, "They were beating us like a yard dog." He remembers walking behind Coach Henderson, coming through the pines, and Henderson said, "We've got them where we want them." Brooks said, "Got them right where we want them? They're kicking our teeth in." The staff went in, made the half-time adjustments, and calmed the players down. Coach Henderson gave the pep talk everyone needed—he simply said, "We're going to go out and get a turnover, and we will stop them. We're going down to score, push it in, and change the whole momentum of the game." Brooks recalls that they went in for the second half and kicked off to Warner Robins, who then threw an interception. One of Clarke Central's players, Jeff Greer, ran the ball down close, and then they ran it in with seconds to go. It was late in the game, 21-14, Clarke Central scored, tied it up, and then it was Warner Robins' ball. It was deep in their territory, they elected to kick, and Coach Henderson instructed the players to block that kick. Frank Battle, a gifted jumper, blocked it. Clarke Central recovered it, and scored to win the game, just like Coach Henderson said they would.

Randy Williams remembers another such time when he felt positive attitude had a tremendous effect on their game. It was 1985, and Clarke Central was playing Lagrange for the North Georgia championship. Williams stated that he was having a really tough time with their defensive tackle. He came off the field, and Offensive Coordinator Coach Ben Scott asked if Williams could block the guys—Williams said he didn't know. Coach Scott didn't look pleased, talked to Coach Henderson, then came straight back. He asked Williams again : "Can you hold him?" and this time Williams said, "Yes, sir." Scott went on to say, "Coach Henderson said you would find a way." Williams WAS able to hold the tackle and not get caught, and David Perno was able to move forward and "do the rest." But what Williams remembers was the confidence they had in him, the positive attitude, and of course, Coach Henderson's grin when he came off the field after the successful play.

Later, Williams worked for Henderson on his coaching staff. He recalls that some accused Henderson of "not understanding enough plays," over the years. After he began working with Coach Henderson, he was privileged to learn firsthand (in what he called a private coaching clinic) about Henderson's vision for the 1992 offense. He says, "Coach called me into his office and told me, 'It's never the plays, but the confidence your players have." He then proceeded to spend the next two hours drawing up four different offensive systems that could feature all of their talent, which Williams said was great that year, with such players as Palmer Bush, Stacey Bailey, Rip Kendrick, and Ricky Smith. They ended up setting the collective single season rushing record in 1992. Henderson also showed Williams a "pro-style" passing attack that he'd been aware of for years. It made Williams laugh, knowing that no one truly knew the depth of Henderson's play knowledge. Plays are only as good as the confidence and character of the players!

But beyond the players, Coach Henderson also worked to build confidence in his coaching staff. After Randy Williams arrived at Clarke Central to coach, Henderson asked him to head up the track program. Williams was surprised, never having been a track athlete, and he brought this up. Henderson said, "You'll do a good job, and get what you need to be successful. Just get me a list of what you want to do and need." Williams was excited about the opportunity and went to inventory the situation. He came back to Henderson just a couple of days later with his list: all new equipment, new uniforms, a new track, and a budget that could support ongoing needs. Henderson asked Williams how he was going to get everything. Williams was even more confused now, and indicated to Coach Henderson that he had said those things would be provided. Henderson replied, "Correct, you will get what you need, and I am confident in that. I just need to know how you are going to get it, and…I need for you to head the girls' track program as well." It had already been announced that Williams was committed to the program, and he said he was "furious" with Henderson, more upset with him that he had ever been. So, Williams got to work, and they had raffles, doughnut sales, BBQS, "you name it…we raised enough money for everything but the new track. We also had over 100 kids involved. Little did I know…." One day, Henderson came to see Williams, and asked him to go to Atlanta to visit then Governor Zell Miller, who wanted to meet Williams. At lunch with the governor, Williams talked about the new track program he was building, how proud he was of the team for raising the money for their needs, and that they hoped to build a new track in the future…maybe a year or so. They went on to other topics, but later, Governor Miller said, "Randy, how much money would it take to get the new track started?" Randy informed him that 25% of the projected cost would enable them to move forward. The Governor then asked if he could help with a contribution. "I about fell off my seat and started eating my ice cream with a fork!" Williams exclaimed. On the way home, Coach Henderson teased Williams by saying, laughingly, "I bring you as a guest and you take over the whole meeting. " Williams says now, "Coach always had a purpose and had never failed to help people who were helping themselves. He saw our low-income athletes working hard, and he set them up for success with that meeting. To this day he has never admitted his hand in that gift…"

John Barnette, Clarke Central student, and later coach with Henderson, remembers being in a coaches' meeting one day, and Henderson says, "We've got an opportunity." He proceeded to say that they needed a girls' basketball coach. John said he was about twenty-three or twenty-four, and he leaned up (being cocky), and he looked around and said, "My mom played basketball." Coach Henderson sat back in his chair and said, "You've got it." Barnette said, "No." Henderson said, "You've got the job." So that's how John Barnette became the girls' basketball coach at Clarke Central.

Charles Bellflower said, "Billy instilled in me the confidence that 'It can be done.' Little did I know that, by heeding the call to get involved with

Clarke Central football, I would later have opportunities in athletics at the Universities of Georgia and Oklahoma and Georgia Southern University. It would also give me a chance to work in broadcasting and politics."

This positive attitude allowed his players to be more accepting in difficult life circumstances. Claudie Brown, quarterback at Willingham, planned to play football at UGA. However, in a practice, another player, Durward Sauls, clipped him, and essentially ended Brown's football possibilities. He never played at UGA, but went on to major in math. However, the positive piece (and attitude) to this tough circumstance would come just a bit later. When Brown was examined for the draft, he was turned down because of his knees. He credits Durward Sauls with keeping him out of Vietnam.

Derek Dooley feels that one of Coach Henderson's greatest strengths is the ability to connect to and positively affect every player. "It didn't matter where they [players] were from, it didn't matter how poor, how rich, what the abilities were, Billy Henderson, more than any person I've ever been around, was able to reach into their souls and get them to be and do things they never thought were possible. That's the true mark of a great coach, and that to me is what made him so special."

Bryan Harris, who's known Coach Henderson all his life, tells of how Coach encouraged him and the other ball boys by allowing them to travel with the team and participate in team activities. He recognized them for their achievements and put their pictures on his wall. Later, when Harris was a player on the team, he walked into Billy's office and saw "a large framed picture of all of us ballboys with Billy kneeled behind us, his arms propped on our shoulders. He pointed to it when he saw me and said 'That is one of my favorite pictures. I look at it all the time and smile. Little did I know then what a man you'd become …'"

CHAPTER NINE

# PERSEVERANCE

*My motto was always to keep swinging. Whether I was in a slump or feeling badly or having trouble off the field, the only thing to do was keep swinging.*

*—Hank Aaron, professional baseball player*

Willingham High School Football Team, 1965

Henderson says, "I set a record in basketball at Jefferson the first year I coached. We played nineteen games and lost nineteen, and the moral of the story is—Don't Ever Quit." At that early point in his career, he had Wright Bazemore at Valdosta as one of his role models. He even put a picture of Bazemore in his wallet, as inspiration and motivation, and carried it until he moved down to Willingham and finally played Valdosta. The first season was a losing season, 0-7-3 record, but Coach Henderson said, "Those kids stuck together, and in a few short years they were whipping Valdosta [and others] three straight." He feels there are many times in life when it seems you can't do anything right, but you've got to keep "plugging away." Fred Johnson, principal at Willingham High School from 1959–1973, remembers this tenacity. "He just didn't quit. I guess you call it stubbornness."

There were other times that may have felt defeating, such as when Willingham had just beaten Valdosta (ranked number one in the nation at the time), and was poised to win the state championship. However, the very next week they were defeated by Jordan 34-13, a huge disappointment, but what did Henderson and his boys do? They just kept plugging away, never quitting. Jimmy Hammond remembers that as a lesson from early on, "He [Coach] emphasized that once you have made a commitment to start something, don't quit. Always finish what you start. Don't let others down, don't let yourself down." Henderson also taught his players that no one really respects a quitter, and that every time someone quits something, it becomes easier to quit the next time, or anytime things get hard.

Again at Clarke Central, in 1975, Henderson remembers they were beaten solidly at the season opener, 21-0, the second game they lost 54-6, the third game they were beaten 28-0. He remembers his wife asking him, crying, after that third game, "What have you been doing over there?" He made a decision then, and the next day, the coaches and players had a rededication, if you will. They had a very hard practice, but it was a "rebirth that was needed at that time," as they had only scored one touchdown in three games. They went on to lose the next game as well, 21-0, but Henderson felt the improvements were there. Finally, in the fifth game they played the number four team in the state, and beat them 13-7. This season defined the meaning of perseverance—a steady persistence in a course of action, despite difficult circumstances. And, Henderson felt this level of determination set the bar for the seasons and teams that followed at Clarke Central. Of course, they had him as a role model. Henderson himself never quit, never gave up—as a young child when his father died, as a teen athlete, as a college athlete at UGA, nor as a coach for forty-five years. He always possessed indomitable spirit and determination.

His players and coaches also have benefitted personally from Henderson's lessons, not just in the winning of games, but with successes in life. Charles Bellflower was a student during Henderson's time at Clarke Central, and went on to college at UGA. "While in school, I had to take Biology 101 four times. I was able to succeed because of the encouragement of Billy. After graduating from UGA, I coached football for one season at Madison County High School. It was my goal to be a coach like Billy, though I felt, because I had never played, I couldn't be one. Once again, Billy told me 'It can be done.' Over the years, Bellflower has gone on to earn a master's degree, serve on the Clarke County Board of Education, work in the athletic media relations office at GSU, in the compliance office at the University of Oklahoma, and finally teach and coach at Stephens County Middle School. Jim Bob Harris, too, continues to remember this important lesson of not giving up. "When the chips are really down, I think back to Coach running those "mile runs" and his favorite sayings of "spit on it" when you thought you were hurt, and "suck it up" when you didn't think you could go anymore. That's good advice for anybody these days!" Harris played four years for Coach Paul "Bear" Bryant at Alabama, on teams that went 42-5-1, winning three SEC titles and two national championships.

Mike Stucka, writer from the Macon Telegraph, wrote recently about a former player, Larry Ballard, who recalled this lesson at one of his darkest times. "Ballard was struck by twenty-one fragments from a Vietnamese mine, worried about getting another disease, and struggling with malarial fever when he kept thinking of Henderson, the athletic director at Willingham High, when trying to recover from his wounds. "I laid there. I thought of Coach because he said, 'No matter what, you never give up.' I could have given up, but it just wasn't in me," Ballard said.

Henderson recalls that he first learned about perseverance, not quitting, from his mother, Mina Jewell Henderson. He remembers that she would walk to and from work in order to save the dime it would cost to ride the bus. This was done in order to save money for athletics, for Henderson to play sports and have what he needed—further underscoring that important life lesson, that if you really want something, the goal IS attainable.

These lessons are ones he has passed on, not only to his players and fellow coaches, but to his children and grandchildren. At the dedication of the stadium in Athens in 1996, Henderson's granddaughter, Stefanie Brooks, talked about her grandfather in glowing terms. She stated, "Granddaddy has always motivated me to do my best and to never give up or quit." His daughter, Fran Hobbs, remembers a time in high school, when this lesson of perseverance paid off for her. In her senior year of high school, she took the presidential physical test at McEvoy High School in Macon, and finished the mile run. She recalls being very proud of herself for crossing the finish line, for not giving up, as she considered herself the "unathletic" one in the family. Her dad was at the finish line waiting for her, though she remembers he teasingly asked the PE teacher her time for the run, and upon hearing it, said, "Do it again." Clearly not afraid of her dad in the way his players were, she replied, "Not on your life!" That became a running joke in the family. But Fran always knew that her dad supported her, and feels he taught her to "never give up," something she takes with her through life.

Henderson's daughter Chris has a particularly moving story about a time when her dad encouraged her to "never give up." She began at the University of Georgia during the summer right after finishing high school, saying "by the grace of God, I got in." She took history that first summer quarter, not passing, and enrolled again in the fall. She remembers, "I went to look at my final grade [that second time], and was just crushed—I did not pass again! I hadn't learned how to study and comprehend. Daddy was going to pick me up that day, because I didn't have a car. It was a cold day, everyone else had gone home." When Coach Henderson arrived to pick her up, he had several coaches with him, whom he was also taking home." Chris said, "Daddy always knew your mood. He just let it go for a little while, and I just sat there not saying anything." Henderson finally asked what was wrong, and Chris burst into tears. "I told him I had flunked history for the second time. I felt like I was wasting tuition money and I was on probation, and it was just a real struggle. I remember bawling in the car. Daddy got real quiet and said, 'Just take it again. It will be alright. This is not the worst thing that will ever happen to you. This will make you stronger. Take it, and figure out a way to pass it.' "Chris went on to say that her dad didn't get mad, he didn't say anything hurtful. "He didn't say he couldn't believe I flunked it, or I wasted all this money, or anything like that. We went home, had the holidays, and from then on, I did better. I just kept getting better and better, and I took it again, and made a B."

Johnny Henderson, Coach's son, also remembers this lesson of perseverance well. "I remember playing football at Georgia [UGA] ...not getting a fair chance to play QB. I drew on what I was taught early on, and that was to accept whatever decision coaches make, and make the most out of opportunities given to you, with a good attitude. (Later, he dealt with being moved to DB and then starting for 3 years). I remember making the Colts [Baltimore] and calling him with the good news, only to be released 3 days before the regular season. Once again I had to draw on what had been instilled in me, and that is, when you get knocked down, get up and go again. So I did. The next year I tried out as a free agent with Kansas City, made it to the last cut. Then I remember Dad driving me to Chattanooga in 1980 at age 23, to begin coaching at UT Chattanooga. He and my mother taught me a work ethic and loyalty...that has served me for thirty-one years in coaching and the business world."

CHAPTER TEN

# SPIRITUAL VALUES AND COMPASSION

*Know ye not that they which run in a race run all, but one receiveth the prize. So run, that ye may obtain.*
*1 Corinthians 9:24*

Henderson Children with Their Mother, Easter, 1961

Coach Henderson's spiritual values have undergirded each segment of his life, and, at every opportunity, he worked to incorporate those in helping and teaching others. He was never afraid to seek out spiritual guidance for himself, personally. He often talked with his pastor in Macon, Reverend Jimmy Waters of Mable White Baptist Church. He remembers getting much encouragement from Reverend Waters during times when things were financially difficult, and sustained much strength from the church itself. In fact, he feels strongly that Mable White Baptist Church helped to raise his five children.

Every year at the football training camp in Jekyll, all players and coaches had a devotional time together. They also had a chaplain that traveled with them everywhere they went, and Coach felt there was no doubt how important this was as a part of the success story—a success not measured so much by wins and losses, but by the number of lives touched in a positive way.

Former Bibb County Sheriff Ray Wilkes says of Billy: "He was a fine Christian man." His players, too, remember this deep spirituality, and how important it was. Bill Falconer remembers the team praying together, with

Henderson in the lead, often. Hugh Laing recalls that Coach Henderson taught him many things, one of which was to put God first.

Coach Henderson's spiritual values were certainly carried over into all areas of his life. He took literally the words, "Inasmuch as ye have done it to one of the least of these..." His compassion and reaching out to others has been shown in many ways. His daughter Fran says, "This man would give the shirt off his back...always giving to anyone...family or friends. That is the one quality I admire the most."

Coach Henderson was not afraid to reach out to others by having them be involved in every aspect of his own life, and his family's life. He said that Fosky, his wife, never knew who he might be bringing home with him, because of his deep-seated belief about the importance of caring for others. At one point in Macon, he brought a player to live with them, as he wanted to have a positive impact on that young man. He was Robert Ogburn, an outstanding fullback on the Willingham team, who later went on to help Henderson coach little league baseball. Not only did he feel it was important to help others for the sake of helping, but it had an added benefit: "If you treat every child on the team in a way that lets him know you care about him OFF the field, he will give you all he's got ON the field." A great example of this, Chris remembers, occurred often with Charles Campbell and his buddy Larry Richards, "the gold dust twins." She said, "They were always in and out helping [daddy], or needing his car to go to the prom. Daddy would let him [Charles] have the car and give him some money."

In serious life events, Henderson was there to offer compassion and teach the players how to show it as well. Bill Falconer, Clarke Central, recalls, "When Daryl 'Bodine' Moore's brother died, he bussed all of us to the funeral. He did the same for James Johnson's dad, and he arranged for players to live with other coaches or players when their challenging home lives made it impossible to live at home."

Another way in which he reached out to others was by helping out financially—and if he couldn't do it himself, he enlisted others to help. For example, finances were always an issue for some students who needed and wanted to go to football camp at Jekyll Island every summer. For those who didn't have the money, the coaching staff would assist them in finding jobs to earn the needed money. Inherent in this type of reaching out is the lesson that teaching others to help themselves is far more beneficial than simply giving the money or assistance needed. Further, Coach Henderson participated with the Big Brother Association in Macon while he lived there, working closely with Clyde Chatman, a Church of Christ minister who was director of the organization at that time.

Willie Green feels that this level of compassion is exactly what he needed to succeed in life. "When I was in school in 1984, I aged out, and couldn't play my senior year. Coach Henderson knew...I had talent. I wasn't a dumb kid, but I was the class clown, and I didn't understand the importance of getting an education until it was too late. I remember Coach Henderson coming to me and saying, 'You can't play your senior year because you've aged out, and I'm going to help you. There's a military prep school in Sweetwater, Tennessee, and it's going to cost you, but I'm going to talk to the coach.' Coach knew I didn't have a lot of money, but he talked to my mom, and they put me on a work scholarship. As a result, I was able to play at this prep school as a high school senior, going up against guys that had graduated from high school and were in transition to college. So we were playing...Tennessee's junior varsity, and all of these SEC schools' junior varsities. I firmly believe if Coach Henderson hadn't found this prep school for me, I honestly don't know where I would have been. I wouldn't have been in the pros, and I wouldn't have played college ball. I don't know if there would have been another coach who would have taken me under his wings and said, 'You've got all the talent in the world and you just need a chance,' and he worked and got me that next chance. I will always be grateful to him for that, because it allowed me a second chance in life. After that I never took it for granted. Thank you, Coach Henderson, for believing in me. Thank you for giving me the opportunity to have a second chance in life when most people wouldn't. For that I am grateful."

On an individual level, Henderson has always reached out to students and coaches alike, offering himself in many ways. Dan Pitts, long-time coach at Mary Persons High School, Forsyth, Georgia, recalls that Billy Henderson reached out to him and taught him much about coaching. They attended coaching clinics together, and a friendship developed through this. This was especially meaningful to Pitts as he had grown up knowing about Henderson. He remembers, "When I was a kid in high school, I would skip school and hitchhike up to Athens to watch Georgia practice, and I remember seeing Billy, though I didn't know him [personally] then." Pitts says that Henderson "probably helped me more than any other person in my career." Pitts retired from Mary Persons with a 346-105 record and was selected to the Georgia Sports Hall of Fame.

As a coach, Henderson was always striving to reach out to all students, not just the athletes with whom he worked. Charles Bellflower, Clarke Central graduate, remembers sitting in the gym for a pep rally in 1979. They were close to Henderson's second state football title, just a game away. What made that pep rally memorable, however, was that Coach Henderson never once spoke about the upcoming game and its importance to the team's winning season, but rather, he talked about students who have no plan in life. He challenged each of them to get involved in wholesome activities, including sports.

Indeed, Henderson's giving was not limited to others. His daughter Carol recalls that he sacrificed a great deal in order to provide them with many opportunities. "In the seventh grade, all the students in the school patrol would go on the Nancy Hanks (train) to Washington D.C. I got to go, and I always wondered how we paid for these things. I found out years later that he had just used that money for me to go on that trip, instead of going to a coaching clinic." Carol thought this was especially wonderful, as the trip broadened her horizons—she saw things, did things, and met people to whom she would not ordinarily have been exposed.

When Coach Henderson began his first coaching job at Jefferson High School, in Jefferson, Georgia, the local mill took great interest in the students. The owner of Jefferson Mills provided a summer recreation program on the mill campus for children ages four and up. Henderson remembers, "We would have a ceremony every day emphasizing spiritual devotions and values and reciting the Pledge of Allegiance and doing a flag salute. " This type of programming influenced Coach Henderson to later start his own programs, including one in Macon, Georgia and then later in Athens. When Henderson moved to Macon, he worked with Agnes Hatcher and the Macon City Council, which allotted $10,000 to start a summer day camp. This was first held in the Willingham High School gym. In Athens, Henderson helped to form the Champions' Foundation, also a day camp for children ages four and older, which offers a positive environment promoting spiritual values, patriotism, physical fitness, desirable habits and skills in sports, and the desire to excel in all endeavors.

# CHAPTER ELEVEN

# RESPECT AND LEGACY

*Coaching is a profession of love. You can't coach people unless you love them.*

*—Eddie Robinson, college football coach*

Billy Receiving National High School Coach of the Year Award, 1972

Henderson believes he learned to respect others from his mother, that she taught him to treat EVERY person like he would want to be treated. This attitude of his mother's, and of his, illustrates why so many people have profound and deep respect for HIM. Ethan Armentrout, player at Clarke Central, recalls, "The selfless attitude was constantly preached to each of us. Coach would always talk about how EVERYONE was important, from the principal to the guy who scrubs toilets. He treated EVERYONE with dignity and respect."

The respect that others have for Coach Henderson has existed from the very beginning of his career. Johnny Stallings recalls what an opportunity it was to coach under Henderson, beginning at the University of South Carolina in 1957. "The next year Coach was hired as the new head coach and athletic director at Willingham High School. He asked me to join the coaching staff, along with Dave Hill, Henry Middlebrooks, Billy Beale, and Martin Allman. This was the beginning of a great tradition at Willingham High School."

Billy Beale, player and later, coach, feels that "I was blessed in my relationships to great coaches. I thank the good Lord that Coach Henderson hired my dad when Willingham was started. I played for Billy Henderson, did my student teaching under Dan Pitts, and have worked for Larry Campbell for nearly 40 years. I'm still coaching baseball, and still find myself telling my players some of the same things that Coach Henderson told us at Willingham." Alan Redmond feels similarly, saying, "I am proud to say that I played for Coach Henderson and that he was my neighbor and IS my friend. Except for my parents, no one influenced my life like Coach did. The discipline I learned from Coach Henderson has carried me through life."

That respect reached far and wide, much to the surprise of some young players. James Holland remembers that, "I was blessed to have been recruited by several schools during my senior year. At the University of South Carolina, I was in the stands watching the game versus Maryland. A couple seated behind me...got into conversation...asked where I was from. 'Macon, GA, I replied.' Later, the man asked, 'Where do you go to high school?' Willingham, I responded. In a few minutes, he asked, 'Who is your high school coach?' I answered, saying Billy Henderson. 'That's nice,' he said. After a few minutes of silence, he tapped my shoulder. He handed me a business card. 'If you can play for Billy Henderson, you can play for the University of Maryland. I'd like for you to come up and visit us.' The man was Warren Giese, athletic director at the University of Maryland. Holland went on to play football for Georgia Tech, with a football scholarship.

Claudie Brown, quarterback at Willingham after Brad Henderson was killed—"Coach Henderson was a great motivator, great coach, and a great tactician. He knew how to get the best out of his players. Coach said, 'Once you play football, it is going to help you determine how you live your life. Your dedication to the game, the friendships with fellow players, and your morals all help to make you a better person.'"

Hugh Laing remembers many of the lessons learned from Coach Henderson. "He taught me to take great pride in what I do, to always look a person in the eye, to surround myself with good people capable of succeeding, but most important, to always take care of the small things...if you take care of the small things, they will take care of the big things. He also taught me to love myself first so I was capable of loving others. Never, never just think of him as a football coach—if that's all he was, he would never have succeeded. He was another father to us, and we were HIS BOYS."

Bill Falconer, Clarke Central Class of 1981, believes that Coach Henderson's greatest legacy is the number of his former players who have gone on to coach the game and "teach his lessons." From Tennessee football head coach Derek Dooley to Frank "Nitty" Bush, defensive coordinator for the Houston Texans, to David Perno, head baseball coach, University of Georgia, he has led by example. This has created a legacy of team building and individual character building that Falconer believes can be passed along for generations, to their own sons and *their* friends. Further, Falconer went on to say, "In my neighborhood in Atlanta, a number of us "Billy's Disciples," are coaching at the Northside Youth Organization (NYO) with kids ranging from age seven to twelve—Chris Morocco, Charles Pledger, Brack Rowe, and myself—four of us, all from lil ole Clarke Central, now in the same neighborhood coaching. We talk about Billy constantly, reminding each other what Billy did from a football, team building, and individual character building perspective, so we can pass these along to our sons."

"When we proposed to have that reunion to honor Coach Henderson—Coach Billy Henderson Day on September 11, 2009—we called up many former players. Each phone conversation, whether we knew the guy or he was from a different time, lasted a half hour or longer, with all of us telling stories about playing for 'The Old Man.' There were six of us who began the Gladiator Foundation: Shane Walls, John Alexander, Ben Egger, Ryan Brinson, Sam Massey, Jr., and myself. Bryan Harris and Bobby Stamps also pitched in with extraordinary help when it got close to the event." The Gladiator Foundation was started by a group of Clarke Central alumni who are committed to supporting the efforts of CCHS Athletic Department. They were the backbone of the event on September 11, 2009, at which 200 or more of Henderson's former players attended on his behalf.

Kicker for the Carolina Panthers, John Kasay, feels, "He still has an impact on me and a great influence. I am still playing football with guys that are twenty or twenty-one years old. A lot of those things I learned from him. He has always been good to me. I can't communicate how thankful I am for how good he always was to me." Kasay's teammate at CCHS, Willie Green, football player at Ole Miss and later for Denver in the NFL, remembers growing up with respect for Coach Henderson. "When I was a kid, Coach Henderson was already well-known. We were brought up in the neighborhood. We knew Coach and we knew of his football teams, and we, as kids, looked forward to putting on that red and gold. You just didn't know him from being a coach; he was sort of like a father figure to pretty much everybody in the community. He was well-respected in both the African communities and the white communities. That kind of gives you the understanding as to why he was a champion in his own right—because he was able to relate to the people in the neighborhood. My mom ran the local recreation park at Jack Arnold (now the boys and girls club in Pauldon), and Henderson would come out to the neighborhood and talk to the kids about football, and about school and life. As a kid, I looked forward to being on his teams because he produced so many championships, and he was well respected in the community." Willie Green isn't the only one who remembers him this way. Jim Bob Harris recalled that Coach Henderson came to the Y when he was young and talked about football. Harris went on to play for CCHS and for Alabama under Bear Bryant.

"Coach Henderson has been an inspiration to so many young men—I don't think you can go anywhere in the state…and not have somebody that knows someone that played football for him, was inspired by him," stated Mike Waldrip, vice-president of operations for Holiday Inn in Athens, and former president of the Touchdown Club of Athens. Jim Bob Harris is just such an example. He said, "I remember in 1977 beating Cedar Shoals and our team winning the sub region championship before losing to Peachtree. That's when we really turned the corner—started working even harder, with a goal of being state champions. And so we did. I remember us beating Lakeside for CCHS's first 8-AAA region title. Then Newnan, S.W. Dekalb and Valdosta! Coach won some more state championships, and a lot more games, but more importantly, *he has always had such a great impact on so many lives.* That's what I remember about Coach Henderson, and that's why I and so many others love him like we do.

Bryan Harris stated, "I think often about how many of the things I do in my daily life were engrained into me by Billy. I still try to show up to meetings 15 minutes early. When things get tough, I picture those large block letters on the wall that read "WE LEAD" and "IT CAN BE DONE." I stand straighter when I hear "The Impossible Dream" and my heart races when "Eye of the Tiger" comes on the radio. Most of all, I know that within each person, there is the ability to be a champion; some just need a coach to pull it out of them. That's what Billy did, regardless of who you were, where you grew up or how talented you were, he saw the potential in each of us to be champions…"

Brian Kemp, currently serving as Georgia secretary of state, saw Billy as a role model and father figure. "He saw potential in everyone, players, cheerleaders, managers, band members, students, and the community. That's why he was so respected and that's why, if Billy said, 'Run through a brick wall,' then we would run through the brick wall!" The impact he had on the lives of so many of us will truly live on for generations!"

Chester Pierce, recently retired teacher, coach, and principal at Mount de Sales Academy says, "Many high school coaches, including Coach Billy Henderson, inspired me to enter the coaching profession. In the record books, we know that Coach Henderson was a very successful football and baseball coach; however, his style of coaching was also a factor in his influence. I was never lucky enough to be part of a coaching staff with Coach Henderson; however, I did stand on the sidelines and sit on the bleachers to watch him work his wonders. His knowledge of both games and his love of the sports were obvious. I learned from Coach Henderson how to demonstrate respect for fellow coaches, players, and opponents. I would like to thank Coach Henderson for his influence over my career decision."

Edgar Hatcher states, "To tell you how much respect I have for him: Since 1968 he has told me to call him 'Billy.' Since 1968, I have never called him 'Billy,' it has always been Coach Henderson." And Charles Bellflower remarked, "My proudest accomplishment as a member of the Clarke County Board of Education was in 1996 when I led the effort to have the stadium at Clarke Central officially named Billy Henderson Stadium." Other players recall the lifelong impact: "I can only say that...I have been a better person and had more success in life by both of their [Henderson and Brad] examples in life. My wish is that I could have one-tenth the success with the impact on people, through living a life of examples, such as Coach Henderson has lived," says Larry Evans.

Legendary coach Vince Dooley, UGA, said, "Billy Henderson was the epitome of the high school coach, teacher, motivator, disciplinarian, confidant, humanitarian, and substitute father. Throughout my college coaching career, as I was on the road so often and struggled to balance the high demands of my job with family responsibility, Coach Henderson was a godsend part-time father to our sons, Daniel and Derek (who played on two of his championship teams) and our two daughters, Deanna and Denise, who supported his teams as cheerleaders. Barbara and I are eternally grateful for the guidance and support he gave our children. He did the same for countless others who had the good fortune of being in his program, which was ultrasuccessful both on and off the field. God bless the Coach Billy Hendersons of the world!!"

Derek Dooley, son of Vince Dooley and now head coach at UT, remarked," I think it is fair to say that, in all my years of coaching, when it came to important decisions with the team or otherwise, it's rare that I didn't ask myself—What would Billy do? He's just had a profound influence on my coaching career, and whenever I'm at a loss for what to do, I always reflect back...so he continues to influence me today in coaching." Dooley also feels that Henderson's impact on HIM, is a great reminder of how he, as a coach, can also impact others—"I'm so grateful that I was able to be touched by Billy Henderson. Hopefully I can have…a positive effect on other people the way he had on me." Derek Dooley's respect for Coach Henderson is so great, that when he won his first bowl game as head coach, at Louisiana Tech (the school's first bowl game victory in twenty years), he gave Henderson the game ball, "I think it's on his mantle in his home now." The younger Dooley has coached at Georgia, SMU, LSU, [where they won two SEC titles and a national championship], for the Miami Dolphins, for Louisiana Tech as his first head coaching job, and is now at the University of Tennessee.

Former governor of Georgia, Sonny Perdue says, "What I remember about Coach Henderson's teams is how competitive our games were. His players were well-prepared and disciplined. But more than that, I respected Coach Henderson because of the way he carried himself, the way he respected the game. Preparing his teams to play a game was NOT his most important role. He wanted his players to be successful in life, and he knew that the way he coached them would impact them forever. He never forgot that, and THAT is what I remember, and respect, more than even the wins and championships."

Larry Brown, Willingham Class of 1962, commented, "I played football for Coach Billy Henderson at Willingham High School. I always felt like Coach Henderson was my second dad. He was a great motivator both on and off the football field. I have always given him credit for the work ethic I have developed—doing the best I can, no matter what I'm doing. Any success I may have had, I attribute to my Lord Jesus Christ and Coach Henderson. Coach will always hold a very special place in my heart."

"Billy was good in everything he tried. He could pick up anything. He was good at it the first day. Billy was a fine Christian man. Billy had a heck of a record and influenced a lot of young boys that were coming through the system as to what they would become. I think Billy Henderson probably is what we really need in our schools today, or people who have the feeling he had for the students and the job he held. Billy was well-known in Macon, Georgia and well-liked," commented Ray Wilkes, former sheriff in Bibb County and classmate of Henderson's.

Henderson's family too, always had tremendous respect for him, even as young children. His youngest daughter, Chris Watts, recalls an occasion on which she and her friends made some prank phone calls from his office. She was eight or nine years old at the time, and remembers him walking in to ask what they were doing. She lied, and said calling friends—he said okay. Later, when she went home, she says she burst into tears and told him the truth, because it just killed her to lie to her dad. She knew he trusted her (and inherent in that, she trusted and respected him). He told her he knew she had lied, but didn't punish her, just told her not to do it again. This was such an important lesson for Chris that it stands out so clearly to her now.

As a fitting tribute for someone who has touched so many lives, a resolution was recently passed in Macon to name an interchange after Coach Henderson. Ed Defore, a friend of Henderson's at Lanier High School, stated, "In honor of Billy's many accomplishments and his outstanding character, Bibb County Commissioner Joe Allen and I, a forty-year member of Macon City Council, along with a friend, M.V. Bostick, have proposed a joint resolution to name the four-lane Sardis Church at I-75 South, the Coach Billy Henderson interchange." This resolution was proposed in October 2010, and the support for it has been tremendous. Mike Stucka, writer for the Macon Telegraph, interviewed a number of former players and friends of Coach Henderson's, all of whom continue to remember the lessons he taught them. He wrote, "Larry Ballard, a retired electrician, thinks the honor proposed Wednesday morning is more than appropriate for a man who may have saved his life." State Representatives Bubber Epps and Allen Peake expect that legislation to name the interchange will pass with no problems.

CHAPTER TWELVE

# MEMORIES OF BRAD HENDERSON

*When you are sorrowful, look again in your heart, and you shall see that you are weeping for that which has been your delight.*

*—Khalil Gibran, poet*

Dickie Maddox, Mike Luzier, Brad Henderson, and Derrell Parker, 1964

Coach Henderson recalls Brad, his oldest son, playing little league baseball. "We were in Atlanta at Buckhead for the state title, Brad was 11. He had another year in little league. In this game, he struck out, and collapsed onto home plate, and went into convulsions [upset that he had struck out]. But fifteen minutes later he was eating his hot dog. He got over it quickly and was getting ready for another sport."

Fred Johnson, principal at Willingham, 1959–1973 remembers when Brad died. "He was killed in a horrible accident. He was just a young high school kid, and his girlfriend, doing nothing wrong. Actually, they were stopped at a stop sign, waiting for the traffic to clear out, and somebody ran the sign from the other side, and hit them head on."

Ray Wilkes, former sheriff, remembers, "It was in the afternoon. It was getting very close to football practice time. I was in the office or either I was on the road in my car. I don't quite remember, but, anyway, I heard that there was a very bad wreck at the intersection of Wesleyan Drive and Riverside Drive. I was chief deputy sheriff, and I went to the intersection. There was a car that was sitting at a stop sign on Wesleyan Drive. It was about to cross but it was waiting. A car came the opposite way. It was crossing the intersection and apparently hit the rise in the road, became airborne and came down on them and killed Billy Henderson's son Brad and the girlfriend that he was with. I looked at my watch and I realized that we had some mobile units of news people who could be on the air in just a few minutes putting this out. I thought I'd better try to beat that unit and get over to the school and see Billy. Well, I gave it the gas and I got to the school and I went to the building his office was in. I saw 'Coach Henderson' on the door. There were two boys out in the hall and I said, 'Is Coach Henderson in?' They said no but he would be back in a minute, just go on in and wait for him. I was trying to get myself prepared to tell him what had happened. When I opened the door, he was sitting at the desk. It shocked me because I was not expecting him to be in there. I walked up and I said, 'Billy, I've got some bad news. I've got to tell you…' and he interrupted me. He said, 'It's Brad isn't it?' I said, 'Yes.' He said, 'Is he dead?' I said, 'Yes.' He said, 'I know.' It was late, and I stayed with him, and some other people came in, and that was about the way it went. It was one of the worst occasions I've ever had to deliver bad news because I wasn't expecting him to be there, and I wasn't prepared to deliver it, and he wasn't prepared to accept it, and it was really a bad day when that happened."

Fran Hobbs, Henderson's oldest daughter, said, "I was twelve years old when Brad died. We were very close. Carol and I were playing at a friend's house when the call came. I knew deep in my heart that something was wrong. My first thought was that something had happened to my mom or dad. I remember putting my arms around Carol and telling her it was going to be okay. We came home to a lot of people scattered outside and inside of our home. There were a lot of red roses that people brought over. To this day, I don't like red roses—too much of a reminder of the day I lost my brother. It broke my heart to see my parents in so much grief. And the pain I felt that day was almost too much. Brad and I shared a very special relationship. I remember the night before he died. We sat outside under the stars, and he was being the big brother he always was. We talked for at least two hours. He told me he was proud of me, and asked me questions about my dreams. He listened as he always did, as I shared my dreams with him. He shared with me his dreams of having a family. He told me he loved me, and after that he kissed me on the cheek and we went inside. Brad was always very protective of me. He stood up for me, and was always there. But the next day he was gone. My whole world shattered. I thought I would die from the pain of watching my parents navigate through it. I thought my loss would kill me as well. I loved him so much. The journey of getting back to life as a family was hard. Trying to live without that wonderful person, the kindest person I knew. He brought so much joy. God has been faithful to bring healing, and allowing us to move forward. I do carry Brad with me everyday."

Chris, one of Henderson's younger daughters, said the one thing she always remembered about Brad was that he tickled her, and "I remember going into the room and he just lit up the room. He was always so good to me, and kind and patient. That was the big thing." She recalled one occasion in which she "cried her eyes out," because Brad got a spanking. She said she was so worried about him, because he was always so nice, and she remembers hiding in her room thinking, "Poor Brad, why are they spanking him?"

"I remember the death of my brother," stated Johnny Henderson, "and wondering how did my mother and father deal with such a tragedy. They always said through faith and belief in God. I didn't know how in the world I could ever live up to that legacy, but playing football in a stadium named after my brother was something I was very proud of."

Larry Evans, Class of 1965 Willingham Rams, recalled, "Brad Henderson was a young talent that we all recognized very early on, and when we heard that Brad and Diane had been killed at a stop sign by a drunk driver, we all went into shock. We have carried that lesson of horror for all of our lives. The nicest couple you could ever meet, and Brad was someone with a talent not only for football, but for living life with a smile on his face, and for being a leader. But, the example that Coach Henderson lived during that very dark period was a lesson we all observed and will never forget."

"Brad was an amazing athlete in all sports. I think his favorite sport was baseball. He signed my yearbook once, Ty Henderson, referring to his favorite baseball player," remembered James Holland, Willingham.

Claudie Brown remembers Brad's tremendous arm, and though he himself played quarterback, safety, and halfback, he knew he didn't have the arm that Brad had. "Brad died in 1964 on Labor Day. We had just come off beating Warner Robins 25-0 on Friday night. The rumors had started Monday while we were gathering for practice. I had heard there had been a terrible accident, but the players didn't know anything. A couple of coaches showed up, then Coach Henderson comes up. At that time the players didn't think they would have a practice. Henderson walks up and says he figured we'd heard the news about Brad and Diane Driggars, they'd been killed in a car accident coming home from High Falls. We thought Coach would say everyone go home and think about what you are going to do, come back tomorrow. But that's not what happened. He told me to get over there and do calisthenics. I questioned this and said, 'What?' Coach said, 'Yes sir, we're a football team. We will deal with the other situation but today we have to prepare for Dougherty County. Let's get after it." Brown doesn't remember Brad being discussed by Coach Henderson again, and the players in turn didn't talk about it. They, of course, went to both funerals, but no discussion was held. Brown stated that he never saw Henderson break down, and the players felt they had to follow his lead.

# APPENDIX

*This is the first of two television interviews which Aubrey Hammack had with Billy Henderson in January of 1994. A third program was done in April of 1996. These are from a Macon television program called "Keeping in Touch," which accented various psychological and social issues in the middle Georgia community.*

**KEEPING IN TOUCH**
with Aubrey Hammack

*Hello and welcome to Keeping in Touch. I'm Aubrey Hammack, your host, and our special guest today is Billy Henderson. We're going to start the program today, I suppose, by talking about some of Billy's accomplishments and as we told him a little while ago at my office, they've been so many that we couldn't possibly get them all in.*

*Billy Henderson was at Lanier High School where he earned 14 letters in basketball, baseball, football and track. He made All American in football two times. He played in the All-Star game in New York coached by Babe Ruth. At the University of Georgia where he attended later, he earned eight varsity letters in football and baseball. He set several bowl and school records and was a three-time MVP in baseball. He also had two seasons with the Chicago Cub organization, which included Macon, Fitzgerald, and Greenville, South Carolina. In his coaching profession, he has coached at Jefferson High School, Athens High, Furman University, the University of South Carolina, Willingham High School here in Macon, where he won the state AAA baseball championship in 1969, and, also, he coached at Mount de Sales, where he won two state baseball championships and was named national coach of the year. Since that time he has won three state championships in football at Clark Central in Athens. He has won three state championships in football, three in baseball, and one in swimming. He is now in his forty-third year of coaching and is married to the former Fosky West. They have four children and eight grandchildren. Billy, that's a lot, that's a mouthful. Welcome to the program today.*

Well, thank you very much and, of course, I owe it all to my background here in Macon, the boys' club many years ago, the YMCA, a great high school at Lanier High School, and all my many teammates and friends, but we didn't mention Brad at that time.

*One of the things before we get started today , this is a two-part program and the second part of the program is also going to be taped today. It's going to be on the death of your son, Brad, and we're going to be talking in great detail about that. That program will be aired a couple of weeks after this program.*
*Out of the accomplishments that are too numerous to mention, what has been the most significant to you?*

As far as player, coach, what are we referring to now?

*For your entire accomplishments over your career.*

Well, I guess you might say some people might think it has to do with winning and losing on Friday nights or the baseball game itself, and it's very important and very stimulating, but the day-by-day contact is probably the most rewarding experience when you are working with young people teaching and coaching. To work with these youngsters and watch over a period of time as their attitudes improve, as well as their self esteem, it is rewarding. Of course, it's easy to teach and coach the fast and beautiful. Like this dear friend in Athens commented not too long ago, some people are born on third base and think they hit a triple. It's easy to work with these people but the demanding and the challenge is to work with these youngsters who are not beautiful, who are not as gifted as others and see them make their mark in life. My most treasured moment was in 1977. Clarke Central was preparing to play for the state football championship there in Athens, Georgia. It was on Thanksgiving Day, 1977. We were in our weight room and, by the way, in our weight room, we've got it modeled after Lanier High School where I went to school and got my start in athletics. "We lead" and "It can be done" is in broad letters on that weight room wall. Our chaplain was there and, as we prayed right before we went to practice on this Thanksgiving Day, we had mothers, daddies, friends, girlfriends and just a wall of humanity in our weight room. The chaplain said his prayer and everybody held hands and I could literally see the hands shaking and vibrating and just tension and every head bowed. I didn't close my eyes. I just watched and that moment was a beautiful moment. I said if everybody in this world would do this and, by the way, there were black hands, white hands, there were rich hands and poor hands and every walk of life was holding hands for a common purpose. I wish to God that everybody in this world could come together for a common purpose. I wish that everybody in this world had common purpose so we could all work together and have no problems.

*You've spent your life working with young people. Why do you think that has come to be?*

Why have I spent forty-three years? That's a good question. Again, I was blessed to grow up in Macon, Georgia, a very progressive town. I was blessed that I wandered into a boys' club when I was 11 years old and I was influenced by that great organization. When I make my first million, a lot of it is going to go to the Macon Boys' Club and, of course, the YMCA with all the leaders there. But when I was thirteen years old, I knew exactly what I wanted to do in life. I was blessed by having some great teachers and coaches at Lanier. Ouida Poe, who was my English teacher taught me priorities—that academics do come first. And Tom Porter, Cotton Harrison and Lem Clark were my role models. Well, there's no question about it, my dad had died when I was eight, and my mother prayed for these people every night because she was grateful that her son had somewhere to go every afternoon to practice. John Stooge Davis was another coach that influenced me and was a near father to me. When I was thirteen years old, as a result of these great men and great teachers and leaders at Lanier, I wanted to play major league baseball. It's obvious I didn't reach that goal because when I was twenty-two years old, I had a poor attitude. I was impatient. I thought I should have been there then but, thank God, I had a mother who insisted that I get a degree so that I could have another profession. But I knew when I was thirteen years old that I wanted to coach and I've been very blessed to be at some fine places to do that.

*You mentioned your mother and I know that you wanted to share the sacrifices your mom made for you.*

I've already mentioned the fact that my dad had died when I was eight. I have two older sisters who live here in Macon, Doris [Lewis] and Kathryn

[DiNardo]. I call Kathryn sister. I have a brother by the name of Red, whose real name is James but everybody calls him Red, who was a professional fighter. That's a story within itself—of what he has achieved. But after my dad died, my mother had to go to work. She walked to and from work every day to save a nickel bus fare (that's how much buses cost at that time) so Billy could play the sports. She would not think of me getting a job because she valued that education. I mentioned the fact that I played in an All American Boys Baseball game in New York in 1945. I believe it was '45, the summer before my senior year at Lanier. I had an opportunity to sign a baseball contract with a sizable bonus. At that time my mother wouldn't have any word of it because she wanted me to get my degree in college. That was one of the best things that ever happened. She sacrificed and taught me values. There is no question about it—she's the dominant influence in my life in a positive way.

*Billy, I know you have a story and I would like for you to share it again about being in the baseball game in New York and Babe Ruth being your coach and something that transpired between you and Babe Ruth.*

That is an interesting story. I remember some of my teammates like Red Wilson, Claude Lewis, and there are so many people I could mention. But I got on a train with a sports writer from the Atlanta Journal. His name was O. B. Keeler. I'd hardly ever been out of Macon, Georgia, much less to New York. Some of my buddies said when I got to New York, I was looking up at those tall buildings and got my tonsils sunburned. The very first night there, we go in this hotel in New York, and we sit at this table at a banquet. I'm sitting next to this guy that has on a pin-striped suit. He is dressed to the hilt, and he is a real articulate gentlemen. I mean gentlemen in the truest sense and, because I was from Georgia, he took an interest in me. We talked and we talked. I'm still shy today, but when I was seventeen years old, I was very shy. But he brought out the conversation in me, and we talked about Macon and this and that and the other. When the banquet was over, I asked one of my teammates who that fellow was. He said that was Ty Cobb. Ty Cobb was coaching the West, and, in my mind, throughout my little boy days, Ty Cobb was the ruthless, vicious, dirty baseball player, but here I'm sitting next to a gentlemen. Now he is like Pete Rose on the field. I mean he is a competitor, he wants to win. Babe Ruth, in my mind, was pictured as a guy you wanted to idealize and follow. It was just the opposite. I had a coach at Georgia who was supposedly mean, but Babe Ruth passed him in every way.

I believe you wanted me to tell you about the incident on the baseball field. There were 25,000 people in the stands, and in the sixth inning, Kurt Simmons, who later played for the Cardinals, was on the mound. The count was three and two on the batter and there were two outs. I knew better, but I got caught in the moment. The base runners were running with the pitch because they had two outs, the ball was thrown. I didn't hear the umpire say ball four and I got that ball. My coaches H. P. Bell and Lem Clark said when you throw one away, throw it away good, and, son, I threw it away. The ball hit the left field fence, and the left fielder got it and hit the back stop with it. The guy who walked scored, and later I told my friends I made the most valuable player for the West. But the very next inning, I'm warming up the pitcher and I throw to second. Then I hear the loudest, meanest, most vicious voice I've ever heard from Babe Ruth saying, "Give me another (some kind of) catcher!" (We can't say it on the air.) So at that moment, and this had a lasting effect on my entire coaching career, but I kneel down to take off the shin guards and chest protector and I can still see tears—it makes me want to cry a little bit right now—falling in the dirt in the Polo Grounds in New York. I defy any of my coaches to holler or shout at my players for making physical errors. Nobody wants to fumble, nobody wants to throw an interception, and no one wants to hit the left field wall from the catcher's spot in baseball. It's okay to holler when they make mental errors, when they don't give 100%. I thought that's very interesting in how we perceive people—Babe Ruth being the idol and Ty Cobb being vicious. It's just the reverse.

*Taking a little bit of a different slant here for a moment, guns, violence with teenagers is a nationwide epidemic. What do you think the problem is here?*

At one time in my life, I used to think there was an answer here or an answer there. It was black or white or this way or that way, but I think one of the major reasons, of course, and I think it's been pointed out by many authorities in your field, is the failure of the home to teach the proper values. I know in the '40s when we went to school and to work that I used to see more trust and faith. I don't have the solutions, all of them, but I do know that people, especially young people, being involved in positive, wholesome, creative activities like I've already mentioned—the boys' club, the Y, athletic programs, the band, and any program after school that teaches values—certainly will help, but until our home situations and family situations improve in America, it's not going to get better.

*Do you think people in sports owe anything back to the youngsters who idealize them and make it possible for them to make some of the big bucks they make?*

We have talked about a book you and I are going to write together one day, and you're going to help me write it. I've seen a lot of changes in these forty-three years, even before that fifty years, of course, going back to when I was a player. All I can speak from are my own convictions. I love baseball and sports so much that I couldn't imagine anyone getting paid to play them. I really felt some guilt the first time I got paid to play baseball because I love it so much. Then you read about contracts of people getting all the money just to play something. Of course, their riches and their careers are very short. I do think it is out of balance, and there is no doubt about it because it is out of balance and because they do get paid even in the college ranks. That's the reason I love high school so much because these kids at that level play through choice. They want to play. They don't have to play. They are not on a scholarship. They come out by choice and that's the purest form of sportsmanship in America today. Paying athletes and demanding all those prices, I started to say probably did make those fans in New Orleans boo their own quarterback when he got hurt, and that was sad.

*We have like a minute to go before we break, but will you tell us some of the things you do to take care of your own mental health?*

Man, I have to work at that. I really do, but that's a simple answer. I recommend to every living human being everywhere I go, every time I speak to a youth group, church group or wherever it might be to do some form of exercise every day. There again, I have to trace it back to Lanier High School in Macon where I got my start—the coaches there, especially John Stooge Davis. He was a physical fitness nut. He was seventy-five years ahead of the game by lifting weights. At one time I used to play handball with people like Tommy Hewlett, who was a tremendous athlete, and Hubert Howell, and there were others. As an adult, I played handball. I started running and then when my knees—as a result of some of the licks I took in football—started acting up, I took up swimming. In fact, this morning I was in the pool at 5:30. There were about thirty other people exercising then because anybody who wants to exercise can do it. It's just a matter of making the time for it, and there are all sorts of opportunities. There's no question about it. Before you start, you're tired and fatigued and depressed, and you exercise. We've talked about this chemistry—maybe you can explain it. You feel a whole lot better and you're better to do a day's work.

*I know we've got to break and we will be right back and talk about your days at Willingham after this break.*

*(BREAK)*

*Billy, what are some of the greatest memories and biggest disappointments while coaching at Willingham?*

There's no doubt about it. We can spend all day, all night and all week and all month talking about the joy and great experiences, not only that I had, but my entire family had at Willingham High School those twelve years. But certainly something that stands out in my mind very vividly was the day I left the University of South Carolina campus. I was an assistant coach there, and I came back home to Macon to help open a new school, A. R. Willingham Senior High School. It was February of 1958, and Dave Hill, who's living here now, and Bob McKinney, who's still coaching, and Johnny Stallings, and others—I could go on and on with the coaches. We talked to every elementary school, we talked to Lanier High School where these students would be coming to our school from, and I'll never forget what a thrill it was in Porter Stadium in mid-February of 1958. We had 175 future Rams to sign up for football, and that was a great thrill. And that great thrill was that first team that we fielded and I was the head coach. But people say, "Billy, you didn't win a game." but you've got to understand when I came from Columbia, South Carolina, we were going to win every game because I knew everything. We got pounded 0-7-3 and one of the most frustrating moments I've had had to do with Moultrie toward the end of the season. We hadn't won a game, and they were piling our little boys up out of bounds. I'm prejudiced hollering at the official, but this time they hit Bobby Mathews, not only a fine football player but he played basketball and was an outstanding pitcher. He was one of my pitchers. They rolled him up on the sidelines in Porter Stadium, and the official was right there picking up the football. I'm in his ear hollering, "Call it, call it, call it!" and he didn't call it. I say, "Gollee!" All of a sudden, I see a red flag. I get his flag and throw it on the ground, and I get in his face and say, "Call it!" Now the official should have thrown me out of the stadium. Of course, by now the players were laughing. I'm thirty years old. They laughed. They thought it was funny, but, sure enough, the official got the football and marched off fifteen yards against Moultrie. Of course, after the game, I have to tell them that wasn't the thing to do. It is the dumbest thing I've ever done in my life, and I haven't done it since, but that's one of the frustrating things I remember. Of course, one of the joys was the first time we beat Lanier. Willingham versus Lanier in 1960. It was 13-7. No way that Willingham could have won the ball game. We ran six plays the first half alone and three of them were quarterback sneaks on my own goal line. But Lathrop Holder and Jimmy Hammond came up for a blocked punt, and we managed to win the ball game. There are so many memories—three straight over Valdosta, six straight over La Grange. All because you had a group of young men who were committed and dedicated and paid the price to be the very best they could be. And of course, there were some other moments that we will talk about later, I guess.

*Loyalty. You're from Lanier. You were Mr. Everything at Lanier. How could you want to beat your old school so bad? Did you have problems with that?*

Whatever I accomplished at Lanier as an athlete or anything else was a result of people around me. Great teammates. Listen, within your own family, you have more of a desire to whip them than anybody else. It was a great feeling to line up against one of my old teammates, Jim Nolan, who's no longer with us. He was a hall of famer, great athlete. No, it wasn't any problem at all. In fact, our Willingham Rams, in the early going, used that game as a measuring stick, you might say. Later, it was Valdosta, but we picked out the very best in the United States and tried to achieve that level of competition.

*Any special memories of Jim Nolan and Goot Steiner?*

Jim Nolan—of course, I've already mentioned the fact that he was a great athlete, great teammate, highly intelligent, and, of course, he was the first young man that dated my wife Fosky years ago. Goot Steiner probably was one of the fiercest competitors I ever competed against. I loved it every time we played, whether it was football or baseball. We were part of forming what is now known as the Lem Clark Baseball Tournament. At that particular time, Goot was coaching at Dudley Hughes, and, for some reason or another, they didn't have spring football practice. So I said, "Goot, how about you being the chairman of the Lem Clark Tournament because I'll be involved at Willingham during spring football?" He said, "Sure, I'll be glad to." Well, the tournament came around and Dudley Hughes and Willingham reached the final game. We got our boys to the baseball field ready to play. We took infield. We took batting practice and were ready to play the game and no Goot and no Dudley Hughes. I said, "I can't imagine Goot Steiner forfeiting any kind of contest. He's such a competitor." By the way, we used to argue thirty minutes before a game just on ground rules alone. So I'm about ready to pack the boys up and carry them back home and say we won the Lem Clark Tournament. I forget which year this was, but here comes Goot. "Where in the world have you been? I can't imagine you forfeiting a game. I was ready to call the Georgia High School Association—Sam Burke and tell him about it." He said, "No, we're going to play tomorrow." He said, "The field is too wet." I kicked the dirt and I said, "Goot, it's dusty. What is it?" He said, "I say we're going to play tomorrow. This is what you get for making me the chairman." He made the decision it was too wet to play and Sam Burke always backs up the chairman. We played the next night, and I'm happy to say that Charles Asbell pitched a one-hitter, and we won the ball game one to nothing.

*One thing I would like for you to do very briefly if you could, is tell us about one young man you sort of took under your wings at Willingham. I think he even moved in with your family. Could you tell us very briefly about that?*

That's right. Robert Ogburn is a lifelong friend. He's an outstanding football player. I think I abused him one night against Lanier. He carried the ball maybe twenty-two straight times, but he was one of those old timey bruising fullbacks who could get you three or four yards off tackle anytime. Of course, the fullbacks at Willingham spoiled me through the years because they could do this sort of thing. Not only could they run the football but, like Robert, could block that end or the linebacker or whatever you needed them to do. But he was an outstanding young man, very bright outstanding student, and we did have the privilege of him living with us for sometime.

*Billy, thank you very much for being on this program.*

Thank you, I enjoyed it very much.

*On this second program, Billy Henderson talks about the death of his son, Brad.*

## KEEPING IN TOUCH
with Aubrey Hammack

*(Music plays as an announcer says: The best record ever, eight wins, one loss, one tie, but 1964 will be remembered for another reason. The Rams' starting quarterback was Billy's oldest son, Brad, a sixteen-year-old junior. Willingham had opened the season with a 25-0 win over Warner Robins. During the game, Brad set a new school record of 173 yards passing. The following Monday was Labor Day—school was out so Brad spent the early afternoon in the company of his girlfriend, Diane Driggars. The Rams had football practice later in the day. Tragically, Brad never made it.)*

*Welcome to the program. As we mentioned earlier, this is a two-part series with coach Billy Henderson, the head football coach and athletic director at Clarke Central High School in Athens, Georgia. As mentioned in the first program that was taped, we talked about the death of his son. This program is going to be one that highlights that time in 1964—Labor Day weekend, exclusively. The whole program will in fact be dealing with him talking about Brad Henderson.*

*In 1964, on Labor Day weekend, tragedy struck your family—your son was suddenly killed in an automobile accident that claimed the life of his girlfriend as well—Brad Henderson and Diane Driggars.*

*Can you reconstruct that day as best you can for starters today?*

There is no question about it; I can reconstruct it just like it happened yesterday or today. It was September 7, 1964, and most of my family was gathered on Westbury Drive right below Westgate Mall. My wife Fosky, her sister and her husband, Ray and Jack, were there, and their children. And the Friday previously we had played Warner Robins and Brad was our quarterback. I might say sometimes it's like the game of golf, and golf is like athletics. Sometimes you think you've got the world by the tail, so to speak, you've got control of it. We had just whipped Warner Robins 25-0. Brad was a straight A student. We talked prior to the show, and you asked me what profession I thought he would have gone into. I feel he would have been a dentist, a doctor, somewhere in the medical profession because every time he would visit Athens or these other places, he would make a point to visit the dentist friends or doctor friends, just to get a feeling of their profession. We had whipped Valdosta a couple of years in a row and it was, you might say, that was one of the highlights of my life at that particular time. I was thirty-six years old, had a sixteen-year old son playing quarterback and September 7 on Westbury Drive, 1964, I'm waiting for Brad to pick me up. He didn't show up at three o'clock, which was uncharacteristic of him. So I decided to walk. So I walked to the school, which was just a few blocks away. Probably didn't have a good attitude about it, impatient, went to my office, and sat down getting ready for the day's practice. Mike Garvin, whom I was later to assist at Mount de Sales in 1970, walked in the door and said, "Billy, two teenagers were killed out on Riverside Drive just a little while ago. So I said right away it was Brad. I picked up the phone ready to dial the hospital and the door was opened. It was Ray Wilkes, the assistant to the sheriff at that time. I looked into his eyes, and I could tell exactly what had happened so I put the phone down and followed him to the car. Then my mind began to wander back to the last time I saw Brad, which was that morning about ten o'clock. He and his buddies Rozie McKinney, Ralph Alligood, Richard Whitfield, (who rode with Brad to the picnic and but did not ride back, but came later) and others, came by. Brad had just got his driver's license in August. He was sixteen on August 15$^{th}$. He would be forty-five today, by the way. So I threw him the keys, and that was the last time I saw him alive. The last time that Fosky saw him alive, she was in the backyard hanging his football uniform out on the line, that she had washed. Brad used to take a lot of pride in the fact that his mother took care of his uniform the best of anybody in the world because she would get a toothbrush and clean the shoes and clean the shoestrings and whatever, and it was hanging on the line. And the last time Fosky saw Brad alive was when he kissed her right on the cheek, and she can still feel it now. I go in the house, I say come with me—and we get in the sheriff's car and we drive to the hospital. We go through this corridor and there, oh, there must have been wall-to-wall people but you don't see them because you're in shock right now. The only thing I have to do at that time is to get to my son, Brad. I did find him, pulled the sheet back, didn't pull it back far enough to see the extent of his injuries but saw him, came back out, saw Billy Beale and Johnny Stallings, and Dave Hill and others on the coaching staff. I said, "What in the world are you doing here? You're supposed to be at practice." So I send them back to practice, I thought. Of course, that particular week we were getting ready for another opponent, but that was the only practice I missed. On Tuesday, we practiced again. On Wednesday, we buried Diane Driggars, our cheerleader. By the way, if I could just a moment give a little history about Diane. Diane was a beautiful girl, not only outside but inside. One of the joys I had was playing golf with Brad, and she would caddy. I've used this on many illustrations with the young ladies in school now in Athens, Georgia at Clarke Central. It would be raining, her hair would be in her face-but she wasn't concerned about her hair, she was oblivious to anything except being happy. She was beautiful both inside and out. September 7th is a memory that will never be forgotten in our family.

*Billy, I know Elizabeth Kubler Ross has written several books on death and dying. She talks about five stages we go through in dealing with death. I think the first stage that she mentions is denial. In looking back when you first heard the word that Brad was dead, did you see yourself in the denial stage?*

There is no question about it—there was a lot of disbelief. You wake up in the mornings and think it didn't happen and wish it didn't happen and pray it didn't happen. Yes, I can see that phase in all of our children, Carol, Fran, Johnny and Chris. Of course they were affected in different degrees depending on what their age was at the time.

*The second stage is rage and anger, according to Elizabeth Kubler Ross. Did you feel rage and anger about Brad being dead after a while?*

You know, I can say with deep conviction that I don't ever remember seeing Fosky in rage or anger. I don't think I experienced rage or anger. As a matter of fact, Fosky sent the family of the driver of the other car a sympathy card just to let them know we were thinking of them, too. I don't remember that stage.

*Correct me if I'm wrong, but was this a head on collision involving alcohol?*

What happened was out on Riverside Drive, Brad and Diane were in the car returning from a picnic with their teammates and friends and cheerleaders. Diane was a cheerleader, by the way. They pulled up at a stop sign, maybe had stopped or were slowing down. From the other direction, this car, estimated to be going eighty miles an hour, went airborne and, just like a missile, came down and hit their car. Mercifully, I understand they were killed instantly. Two lives snuffed out just that quickly.

*We are told that one of the stages of death that we go through is bargaining with God. Please don't let this be—take this back, I'll do anything, God, if you just make this not so. Did that happen with you?*

There again we were blessed. I know Fosky had a spiritual background. This is resolution. There is not enough money in the world to measure how valuable is my mother's faith. I've already mentioned in a previous show, my dad died when I was eight. My mother went to work, and she taught me these words of persistence, dependability, and responsibility. Any valuable trait that I got, I got from her. She walked to work back and forth to save bus fare so I could play. She was busy, so busy working, working for me, letting me know she loved me that she didn't go to church, but I saw her reading her Bible every day of her life, and she would quote me scriptures. At that time, when I was a little boy, I didn't know they were scriptures. Everything happens for the best, which I didn't understand, Knock and the door will open, seek and you will find. All these things are valuable to any person in time of misfortune. Of course, another thing is that we were blessed with a great church there at Mabel White, Jimmy Waters. We will always be indebted to his guidance and counsel. I had some dear friends who came through. At that particular time on the coaching staff, Mack Edwards, Dave Hill, I've already mentioned Jesse Duckworth, Tommy Mixon, who now scouts with the Dodgers, Eddie Battle. I could go on and on, but there are a lot of resources that we have that we have to call on, but in the final analysis we have to do something ourselves.

*You mentioned earlier at the office when we were talking about this that you went through a period of depression, and you could almost remember the day when you saw certain things happen and you saw the sunlight, but the depression sort of stayed with you a while.*

Oh, that is so real. I mentioned to you this morning in your office that, during a four-year period, I must have joined a record number of organizations in Macon—the Macon Coliseum Building Authority, hospitals, Big Brothers, Boy Scouts, YMCA. You name it, I got involved with it, just to stay busy, just so I could come home at night and be fatigued enough to go to sleep. I didn't mention this, but I'd go around to each one of the bedrooms—Chris, Fran, Johnny, and Carol, especially Chris, who was four years old. It would be very desirable if we had that childlike faith that she has now at thiry-three, but I'd go in, and she would say a prayer. She put her hands around my neck. I can still feel her little arms and, without hesitation and through complete faith, she would say, "God bless Diane and Brad up in heaven." She believed then, and she believes it now. There are all sorts of forms of depression. I guess from somebody somewhere we should have gotten counseling at that time, but we didn't. Somebody said stay busy and that's good advice because it's good to stay busy.

Somebody said get physically involved, and I played a lot of handball. At that particular time, I would go out of my way to play tons and tons of handball with great athletes. I mentioned Hubert Howell, and by the way, before I leave, I'll call one of them or both of them and challenge them to play a game of handball. But there is no way to measure what that fierce physical competition did during that era. It without question helps.

*There was a certain day that you remember vividly when the sun came through in your station wagon out at Westgate. That was your time of acceptance, I suppose—the final stage where we accept that somebody is really gone.*

Yeah, I got off track just a little bit, but I'm back. It was four years later. It was in the spring, probably the spring of 1968 or '69—somewhere in there. I had my baseball uniform on. If I did one thing right as far as my family was concerned, we had a little family devotion every morning at 6:30. Johnny didn't particularly like it because he didn't like to get up that early. Another thing, wherever I went, they would go with me. They wanted to go, and I am glad of that. They thought they were fortunate that Daddy had a key to the gym and all their buddies could go to the gym. I was parked at the Westgate Mall. I had my baseball uniform on. Willingham had a game down at the park, Luther Williams Park. All my children were in the car and, for some reason, I can feel sun shining in my face right now. Maybe that was the day. I remember that very vividly. The sun—how warm it was and how great it felt. I always enjoyed putting that baseball uniform on, whether it was as a coach or player.

*Was there any particular member of your family who seemed to have had a harder time with Brad's death?*

Alright, Chris was no big effect. Johnny was eight...don't think so—Carol no—but Fran was twelve years old and most impressionable of all the children. She's forty-one years old now. Talking with the other children and through the years in talking to Fran, she actually had nightmares. She was more affected than all the others of the family and she has actually gotten counseling for this. She lives in Wilmington, North Carolina and her husband is a high school administrator there.

*Billy, I know that we're going to break, but we will talk some more...we will be right back.*

*When we left a moment ago, we were talking in connection with one member of the family who was having it rougher than the others and still has through the years, which Billy mentioned as Fran, his daughter who is forty-one.*

*One of the things that we wanted to talk about was how people responded. People do respond in different ways. I think we mentioned earlier while we were on break that death is taboo....we can talk about anything in the world but people really clam up when we talk about death or somebody just dying. That makes it more difficult for those who are expressing losses, because they have a real need to talk with people and be heard, in connection with someone who has just died. Did you find that to be true when Brad died?*

No question about it. My experiences have told me that you can be with the closest of friends, people in your church, and they are hesitant to mention any subject close to it. Anyone who has experienced the loss of a child or a loved one, for that matter, enjoys talking about this person. I thoroughly enjoyed discussing Brad. When he was ten years old, we sat on the steps in Columbia, South Carolina and could talk on any subject. We played golf together. This is one of the things, especially after his death, that I learned. When someone suffers a loss, any loss, you don't have to say a word to the person. Just go in your presence and tell that person you care and you are concerned. I remember after Brad was killed—I've already mentioned some of their names—there were those that would come and be near. Tommy Mixon was one of them, Jesse Duckworth, Johnny Stallings, and the others,

Eddie Battle, Wayne Beville. Just the fact that someone was there and cares. As years go by, it's been several years, many years...you enjoy talking about it.

*Do you remember when people said the wrong thing?*

Oh, there is no doubt—and I have to share this. I'm sure anybody that has lost a child—to hear somebody say it's God's will. God has a will for our lives, but he doesn't will us to get killed in an automobile accident. That's a deep subject within itself, and I'll just leave it there. Also another statement—well, you've got other children. That's true but that one person was very special, and nothing could replace that person. Those are two things that through the years we've discussed.

*There were other people who were around that were very special to you.*

Fred Johnson, the principal at Willingham when I was there. You might say he was a stabilizing force for me because I've been known to have energy and to jump here and there. Fred Johnson was an ex-commander in the Navy. He was very calm under turbulent water, and, like I've mentioned earlier, an atom bomb could explode behind him, and he may or may not blink. He's not going to get in a hurry about it and not going to make any rash decisions. A great leader, and I appreciate him very much.

*Billy, after the death and you probably have the dates, I don't have the dates, a new football stadium was built here, and it was named after your son. How did that make you feel, and how did it make you feel the first time you went on that field with your players to play a game?*

Yeah, you know Clarke Central played Southwest of Macon in some games. When we go on that field, yes, it is a special feeling. When I hear someone say Brad Henderson Memorial Stadium, it's very special.

*What are some of the memories of Brad that are very special that you don't mind discussing?*

Oh, there are lots of them, and I'll maybe share one or two. Baseball was one of his passions, too. He was eleven years old, and the Macon Little League was playing at Buckhead for the state championship of Georgia. Macon was behind by one run and the bases were loaded. There were two outs, and Brad was at bat. He got two strikes on him and the count went three and two, full count. The next pitch, swoosh down the middle, and he swung and missed and struck out to end the ball game. He collapsed. Brad collapsed on home plate, and I mean he was having convulsions. These psychologists who say that competition is not good for children would have had a field day watching him. But they didn't see him fifteen minutes later in the car drinking his Pepsi Cola and eating a hamburger, getting ready for football season. Competition is great. Of course there were other moments, but that was very special.

*In looking back over Brad's death today, what are some of the things that you feel like that helped you the most in handling his death?*

Well, there's no question about that, and we've discussed that in your office—my mother's faith and what she taught me from the time I was a little guy, that things do happen for the best. I didn't add that it depends on our attitude and how we deal with what death is to us. There is no question about it, we as human beings grow mentally, and we're not going to grow mentally unless we read and study. We can grow physically, and we're not going to get great endurance and strength and good physical stamina without running or some form of exercise and going beyond your limits. But by the same token, we grow spiritually by going to church, Sunday School and all that and all the support groups that go hand and hand with it. And you can't measure friendship and people who really care. So all of that and that's all I can do is speak from personal experience. Jimmy Waters, the church, Beach Haven and all those things played a role in the comfort of our entire family.

*One of the things, I know, that impressed me when I approached you two or three months back about doing this program, one of the first things you said was, "Could we talk about the death of my son?"*

Aubrey, I certainly was very open to that and even suggested that we have a special program for that, which we have done today.

*For the person who might be watching the program today and who has recently lost a child and been through something like you've been through, what would you have to say to them?*

Well, I have been in that position in Athens during the past twenty-one years. It doesn't seem like twenty-one years have passed since we left Macon to go back to Athens. Number one is to stay busy, not necessarily in this order. If you feel like crying—cry. If you feel like hollering—holler. If you feel like you want to get angry and hit walls—hit walls. I remember when they removed my mother from her little apartment on English Avenue, I stayed in there for an hour just hitting walls and crying and shouting because I knew the kind of life she lived. But stay busy, talk to other people who have experienced the same situation. Somebody said it more wisely than I—that this too shall pass. As far as the feeling, it will never go away. Don't ever think it will go away but it will certainly get better.

*You know at times in our society, men are taught not to cry. Well, it's been handed down for a long time. We're supposed to be macho and tough and not let go and shed tears. What would you say about that?*

I think we were teaching youngsters wrong and I'm sure that somewhere back early in my life, I had heard that someone told me the same thing. When I crossed the Stribling Bridge over the Ocmulgee River this morning, I cried a little bit. I'll be talking to some of my players now and through the years and tell them I'm about to cry, and I say I don't apologize for it. I can hear "The Impossible Dream" being played or sung, and I'll cry. I can see the flag being raised, and I can cry with every emotion. I think it is good mental health to show your emotions, whether it's tears or anger or whatever it might be.

*I know this has been a painful voyage for you, to come back and talk about this today. Why were you so willing to talk about this because you even said, "Aubrey, can we talk about Brad?"*

Well, you know we discussed that earlier. I think this is one of the fallacies of people who have lost loved ones, especially children. You love that subject and it is good to discuss it. One of my favorite subjects in life is Brad. I appreciate the opportunity to come back to Macon, where we got our start.

There is no way I could ever repay some of the people at places like the Boys' Club, Lanier, Mount de Sales and other places. It's been a part of our lives, a very positive part of our lives.

*We've talking about so much information, have you seriously considered writing a book? You certainly have all kinds of material. You could write a book on Brad's death alone.*

Well, we've got a lot of notes on yellow pads. I've got boo coos of files way back from Willingham days. That would be one of the privileges. Of course, people ask me about retiring all the time. Little ladies in the pool up at Athens YMCA. Right now, I feel great. I look forward to where I'm going every morning. When the time comes where I don't feel good, when it's not fun anymore—when the times comes and I don't feel like it, I think I'll be the first to know I'm not effective with the young people, I could consider retiring and, at that time, what I'll do maybe is to come back to Macon in some capacity.

*Billy, in closing and ending the program today, going back to the grief and all that your family has experienced in the loss of your son, are there any comments you would like to make that you feel like might help somebody else who has just gone through what you went through?*

Yes, stay busy, show your emotions, and try to think of other people. When I think of myself period is when I get in trouble. Think of other people and give of yourself. No question about it, because those things will help and even doing those things will be painful. You've got to accept the fact that it's going to be painful. Other people have gotten through it and you can too and if things really get bad, get in counseling somewhere. No question about it, you have to go on again being the head of the household and that responsibility. I don't know why somebody didn't suggest, of course they knew we were involved in a church, but no question about it, professional help will be advised.

*Thank you very much for being on the program.*

Thanks, I enjoyed it.

*This is the third of three television interviews that Aubrey Hammack had with Billy Henderson. This aired in April of 1996.*

## KEEPING IN TOUCH

with Aubrey Hammack

*Hello and welcome to Keeping in Touch. I'm Aubrey Hammack, your host. Our special guest today is Billy Henderson, who is head football coach and athletic director of Clarke Central High School in Athens, Georgia.*
*Welcome to the program, Billy.*

Thank you very much, Aubrey. I've looked forward once again to visiting with you.

*I guess for starters, what we're going to do today with the program, is call this Billy Henderson and some memories. We're going to be talking about a lot of different areas and a lot of different names of people that he's been associated with over the years in coaching. And, Billy, maybe today for starters, you have a member of your family who has done rather well in the boxing area that we've not talked about before. Tell us about that.*

That's exactly right, Aubrey, and that's one of my favorite topics. My brother James, but better known as Red, is four years older, and when I was eight, he was twelve. At that time and we talked about this before, and that's why my mother was so high on the boys' club and thank God for the boys' club, because she knew that her two sons were somewhere every night in a positive instructive environment. But my brother had 115 fights. Red had 115 fights in the ring and an untold number outside the ring. He just about fought every day when he was twelve or thirteen. This is another example of why it was so important that adults in the community, like the boys' club, the YMCA and all of these tremendous organizations go hand-in-hand with helping develop these youngsters. A lawyer by the name of Horace Vandiver took an interest in my brother Red and put his hand on his shoulder and said, "Boy, you don't need to fight in the streets. Let's join the Golden Gloves." That's what he did, and very shortly he won the Southeastern States Welterweight Championship, when he was sixteen, maybe fifteen years old. He joined the service when he was late sixteen and was stationed in Brazil.

He knocked out the heavyweight champion of Brazil when he weighed 175 pounds, when he was about seventeen years old. He was very aggressive. If the guy didn't know it, the buzzer would sound, and Red would sprint across the ring, and he would be hitting the guy as he stood. He dropped out of school at thirteen and this is what I preach to young people that don't believe you can achieve anything in life: If you are really determined to do it, you can. When he was thirteen years old, he dropped out of Lanier High School in the eighth grade. At twenty-two years of age, he got out of the service and came back to Macon in '45 or '46, when all the boys were coming home. At that particular time, he took some GED tests and got his high school diploma and went to the University of Georgia. How he did it, I'll never know, but he finished his degree in three years, got his master's and later, he was the assistant to the president of Furman University, the administrative assistant, and, of course, he was a principal two or three times. But more important, his favorite thing in life was teaching in Atlanta. But he died two years ago.

*I know that you had a special relationship with a list of people that you coached at Athens High School, years before you were at Willingham in Macon. One of those was Fran Tarkenton, and you've got one or two stories that you can tell about Fran, particularly relating to baseball. Would you share that with us?*

There's no question about it, Fran is one of the all-time great dynamic leaders. He was not blessed with all the athletic ability in the world. In fact his brother, Dallas, was a much better athlete, but somehow Francis had an overabundance of confidence, which exuded into his teammates and just magnified the whole team. We were playing in Sanford Stadium, and I was coaching with Weyman Sellars. I believe we were playing Elbert County. We were behind 18-14, and this was characteristic of Francis. People talk about teaching him this and teaching him that, he scrambled when he first came into the world. He dropped back to pass. We were behind four points. He got trapped, ran to the right, left and finally a mass of humanity converged on him. I looked at Weyman, and Weyman looked at me and I was head coach. We said, "Oh, my goodness!" Then we heard this tremendous roar from the crowd, and somehow Francis had lateraled the football through that mass of humanity. The slowest guy on the team, I could still outrun him now, Buffalo Smith, got the football and won the game. The clock had ended the game during the play. But Francis was fantastic. He was a pitcher in baseball, led the team in scoring in basketball, but more importantly when he got under center, nobody ever did it better.

*In a baseball game, I think you told me you had to pull him out. He was pitching and he lost control. What happened?*

That was a good one. His buddy Chester Leather was the first baseman. In fact, I saw one of Francis' teammates the other day in the YMCA in Athens working out. We were talking about this incident. Francis was a ninth grader, and the catcher hadn't caught one in about two innings. They hit everything that came up. So I went out to pull Francis from the box, and I got the ball from him and was waiting for him to leave. He didn't know what to do, and he went over to Chester and said, "What do you do when you get knocked out?" This had never happened to him before.

*That's interesting, Billy. I know that when you first started coaching at Willingham in 1958, when you put that program together, there was a coach at that time who came and talked to you about a job. He coaches right up the road in Forsyth today.*

Dan Pitts, one of my all time favorite people. I first met Dan in my first coaching position there in Jefferson, Georgia in 1951. Dan had just graduated from Lincolnton High School and was working for another dear friend, Carol Bufford, whom my middle daughter was named after. Carol Bufford took a tremendous interest in Dan. He, like a lot of coaches, became a second father. I called Dan when I first got the job at Willingham in 1958. He was one of the first people I thought about. He had just graduated from Georgia. In fact, Dan and I verbally agreed that he would come and coach here, but somehow or another, he went back to Forsyth and got the job there. And by the way, he has made a remarkable record. I know that so many people are so proud of Dan.

*I know that he has broken the 300 mark, and we know about that. You're pushing that yourself. What are some of your thoughts about that? You've got, I think, 286 now. We've talked about this before, and you said, "Aubrey, I try not to think about those kinds of things." It has to cross your mind. Will you be relieved when you are over that mark so you don't have to the pressure yourself? When you start thinking about that, is it better to go on and get rid of it?*

Aubrey, that's a benchmark. Wayman Creel was first to get to that mark at the high school level, and Lakeside was the first to do it. There have been two or three others to do it since then, including Nick Hyder, my friend in Valdosta, and the Dalton coach is another good friend. But, no, it's not that important. It's the day by day, week by week working with the kids that's the most important thing. I would not even know how many I've won had it not been for Gary Ford and Charles Bellflower, a guy in Athens.

*Billy, we're going to take a break.*

*I know you are closing in on the 300 mark, and we were talking about that when we left for break. I think you have 286. Conceivably you could actually do it in the next year. That would be putting a lot of pressure on you.*

I don't think anyone would put more pressure on you than yourself. I had a mental block a minute ago when I was trying to think of the other person who had won more than 300, and that was Bill Chappell of Dalton, another dear friend. While 300 is a hallmark and it's a landmark, it's not a real vital thing for me to do as one of my personal goals.

*I'm going to throw out some names of folks that you're very familiar with and have been for a long time and would like some of your comments about some of these people.*
*Bobby Ross.*

Oh, Bobby Ross is one the nicest human beings I've ever met, a real gentleman. We used to spend a lot of time in the weight room in Athens just talking and sharing. We've got a lot in common, personal wise and professionally. I never shall forget, whatever season it was, but it was a disastrous season for Tech. Shawn Jones was a sophomore. Bobby Ross was an example of a coach, starting with little leaguers, of not giving up on youngsters and building confidence. It seemed like Shawn Jones was averaging four or five interceptions a game. He couldn't do anything right. People were down on Tech and Bobby Ross and Shawn Jones. But Bobby Ross stuck with that young man and demonstrated patience, exuded confidence into him, and, of course, it's a matter of record that the young man led Tech to a national title in a very short time thereafter. So the moral of this story is, don't give up on them.

*Tommy Lasorda and Tommy Mixon.*

Tommy Lasorda spoke at Middle Georgia College not too long ago. I was fortunate enough to go down with some men, friends from Athens, Georgia. I've never heard a more interesting speaker than Tommy Lasorda. He kept people enthralled for more than an hour. More than 400 people came. And, of course, Tommy Mixon was personally responsible for getting Tommy Lasorda to speak at Middle Georgia College in Cochran. Tommy is one of the great athletes ever to come out of Macon. I had the privilege of coaching with him there at Willingham. A tremendous competitor, and, of course, when you play any kind of game with anybody like we used to play softball during P.E. classes, and a line drive would hit Tommy's left or right, he was going to dive for it. I consider him a dear friend. I'll always be grateful for Tommy after Brad was killed because he was always there as a support group, you might say.

*Wright Bazemore and dead cats.*

Wright Bazemore initiated me when I was a fledgling coach at Willingham. I shall never forget we played them the first time in 1960. We played them again in '61 and we played them again in '62. By that time, I'd put a picture of him in my wallet that I looked at every day. In the meantime, we were learning at Willingham. If you knock people down long enough, if they've got any gumption at all, they're going to get up. Learn how to block, learn how to tackle, and learn how to execute, and finally in 1963, we won the first game. In '64 we won the second game. We went down to Valdosta and won that game, and in 1965, big game right here in Macon. Oh, big time game. We were playing Valdosta. We tore them up that night 12-7. I shall never forget, we were behind 7-6. We were driving with less than two or three minutes to play, and we had run twenty-three. Twenty-three is a dive play to the left halfback, the old split T. Derrell Parker was an outstanding person, Gary Hutchinson was the quarterback, Ralph Alligood was the full-back, Dickie Maddox and others, but, anyway, Derrell must have run the ball seven straight times. We drove eighty-five yards, and he was holding up his hands. His hand went up, and I thought he meant twenty-three, and I sent in twenty-three. Finally, he ran into the end zone exhausted and we won the ball game. Now the next week—

*Now Valdosta was rated the number one team in the nation and it was triple A at that time.*

That's correct and all we had to do was go to Jordan the next week in Columbus.

*Which had not had a tradition of winning?*

Oh, they were 4-5.They whipped us, and the next week I had to go to Athens and watch Athens High play Valdosta for the state championship. This was '65 but, backing up, the next week after we whipped Valdosta, I got letters from the Humane Society giving me credit for hanging dead cats on underpasses as the fans came in from Valdosta.

*Now none of the Willingham fans did that. You didn't have anything to do with that, did you?*

I'm going to give them the credit for it.

*Vince Dooley.*

Vince Dooley is a remarkable man. Back in the '60s, I had three opportunities to go with Coach Dooley. He's one of the remarkable men of the coaching profession. I was just in his office the other day going over plans for Georgia's D-Day game to be played in our stadium, due to the fact that the Olympics are coming in and they're getting the stadium ready for soccer. But as I stood up in the Butts-Mere Building and looked out over that beautiful facility—no telling what that building cost—you could see the track, the coliseum, the practice area and all the athletic facilities. Of course, he had been in the leadership helm since then, but he makes tough decisions. He's very sound, and I've never called on him when I was at Willingham, Mount de Sales, or Clarke Central when he was not supportive there of the boys and girls. Tremendous human being.

*Tommy Hinson.*

Oh, when I think of Tommy Hinson, I think of somebody as a linebacker who was born to be a linebacker. He wasn't that big. No, probably 160–165 pounds but he was quick, had good balance and had that instinct. He probably made more clean tackles and, when I say clean tackles, that's when coaches teach you to put your nose right there in the guy's numbers and up through his chin and go out the top of his head and lock up. Tommy was one of the better football players we ever had in my career.

*And there was a sad story involving his dad, and it had to do with him getting his law degree, I understand.*

There's no doubt about it. Tommy's daddy was gunned down right outside the police department, and it was a tragedy.

*He was a detective.*

He was the chief of detectives, and he had a prisoner. Somehow, whoever was supposed to search him did not search him, but Brad and Tommy were the closest of friends. I never shall forget; this is a personal humorous story. It seems Brad and Tommy went in one of the dime stores at the mall and it seems that they had some marbles that didn't belong to them. So to make it short, we found out about it, and Roscoe (that's Tommy's daddy) and I found out about it. So we get Roscoe to come in a police car and pick up Tommy and Brad and let them spend just a little time in this half-way house or detention center. They got the message and it didn't happen again.

*Carson Hardison.*

Carson was a halfback at Willingham and a physical specimen, outstanding young man in every way. And of course he could have played a lot of major football.

*And was killed tragically in the Vietnam War.*

That's correct.

*Jim Nolan.*

Jim Nolan and I were teammates. We called him Spider. He played center on the basketball team and center on the football team. In fact, my wife's first date as a youngster was with Jim Nolan. He was an all-time great athlete, dear friend.

*Billy, one of the things that I was wondering about—in 1960–1961, the New York Yankees were king in major league baseball. Were you a Yankee fan? I know baseball was your first love.*

Certainly I followed them and admired them very much. Through the years, every youngster, as you grow up, got the cards and the percentages and whatever, but every major league team was one of my favorites, you might say.

*I know you played at the University of Georgia, and I even have some clips you sent me sometime back where you played halfback. Any special memories that you would like to share and any specific games that you'll never forget while playing in Athens?*

Well, as I look back, one of the highlights of my whole life was being backup for Charlie Trippi, who was an all-time great baseball and football player. The times he would come out of the game, I had the privilege of relieving him, and, of course, during the week, during the scrimmages, Coach Butts would not dare let Charley Trippi get hit. He would let me take all of his licks for him, which was a privilege. I can't cite any one real experience in a game that was highlighted over others.

*But you played in some of the major bowl games.*

Oh, we played in the Orange Bowl. I remember playing Texas in the Orange Bowl, New Year's Day, 1949. I heard this song, and I thought it was "I've Been Working on the Railroad" but it happened to be their theme song, of course, their fight song. We played in the Gator Bowl and we played in the Sugar Bowl.

*What was the hardest hit you've ever taken in football?*

The worst lick I've ever had on the football field occurred this October. We were preparing for winding up the season, getting ready for the playoffs. This was at Clarke Central, this October 1995. We were scrimmaging, and, like all coaches, I was behind the offense. I usually get far enough back, and I've been hit enough to know better, but obviously I got too close. The last thing I remember, the OB rolled to his right and then to his left, and the next thing I knew, I get hit on this knee, and I'm up in the air, and I see the sky. Then bodies of football players are coming at me like bullets, airplane bullets, and the next thing I know, I'm on my shoulder. It still hurts, by the way. I feel the kids getting around me in a quiet sort of way. It seemed like a minute, but it was probably more like ten seconds. I get up and start slapping people on their headgear. It was okay, and the next morning, I couldn't get out of bed—had to call two of my players to come pick me up and take me to Georgia's team physician. I found out I had broken a bone in my leg and had a rotator cuff damaged. That's the worst lick, which includes four years at Lanier and four years at Georgia.

*Billy, I know your tradition has always been a crew cut and obviously you like it; you're proud of it, but you've got some stories to tell concerning your haircut.*

Actually, it has been a convenience. I used to have long black hair like yours, and my good friends would say it would just wave in the breeze when I'd run. When I was at Athens High, my first coaching job, I got this crew cut. During the Vietnam War, it became popular for people to burn draft cards and burn the American flag. This was wrong on my part, but I judged people who had long hair and facial hair, with people who were burning their draft cards. I didn't like it with all of our young men—Carson Hardison and Terry Jackson and others—who had died in Vietnam. During the '40s, we had abundance of patriotism. As a result of these feelings, I'd get three barbers out in front of the Willingham gym and cut their hair. Wayne Jones had a head full of blond hair, probably down to midway his forehead. I told Wayne, "It's got to go." Boy, he cried, tears running down his cheeks. He said, "I'll get it cut but it will not make me a better football player." That stuck with me, and I tell these people who judge others now that you have to look at someone's heart. As I got out of my car twenty-three years ago behind the gym at Clarke Central, there were about eight or nine guys over by their car.

*That's when you went up there to take the job at Clarke Central?*

That's correct. My first day on the job, and they looked at this crew cut and I could hear them say, "Oh, my God!" Another one said, "He won't last a week." I said, "I won't bother yours if you don't bother mine."

*Baseball, going back to baseball for a few minutes, I know you been coaching baseball for a long time. Have you coached baseball longer than football?*

Every job I've ever been hired to do starting with Jefferson was football. This is what I tell young assistants right now. I didn't invent this system, but I was hired to coach football because, for the most part, that's where the gate receipts are, and they support all the others. But when I went to Jefferson or when I'd go to Athens or Furman or South Carolina or even Willingham and later Mount de Sales and Clarke Central, it was important that I be involved in baseball. I haven't coached baseball since 1982.

*I guess you keep up with your baseball record just like you do your football record. What is your baseball record?*

Aubrey, I couldn't tell you.

*Could you give me a ballpark figure?*

It's over 300—of course I've coached American Legion, I've coached Little League, high school and college, but I could not tell you exactly.

*Watching games, do you do a lot of that?*

I'm not a real good spectator. I like to be a spectator when it really gets involved, like the NCAA Tournament going on right now and the World Series and things of that nature, but I like to play or coach for the most part. Unless something is really riding on the game, no, I'm not a good spectator.

*I know it's almost time for our program to end today, but I know one of the things that we had talked about before was the school name changes here in Macon. We were talking a few nights ago when I called you in Athens about some of your feelings about that. I think we've got about sixty seconds left. What are some of your feelings about that?*

I'll be as brief as I can. I think it was a tragedy because there are so many people who cannot identify with Lanier again. I was one of them. Willingham was one of the more recent ones.

*So it made you angry because you went to Lanier?*

That's right, and you've got Mark Smith. Within their own right, they had a tradition that was wiped out and there again is a testimony for athletes. In Athens High, the same way—the Athens High Trojans. They suddenly didn't have an identification. Success in athletics helps to unite communities and I'm just privileged and overjoyed that I have been a part of athletics and this tradition for forty-five years.

*Billy, thank you very much for coming down and doing the program again. I know it's been almost 2 ½ years but I thank you very much for being on our program.*

Thank you very much. It's been a pleasure.

## BILLY HENDERSON'S FOOTBALL COACHING RECORDS

(This information from Georgia High School Football Historians Association)

| Willingham High School | |
|---|---|
| 1958 | 0-7-3 |
| 1959 | 6-4-0 |
| 1960 | 5-4-1 |
| 1961 | 7-2-1 |
| 1962 | 6-1-3 |
| 1963 | 6-2-2 |
| 1964 | 8-1-1 |
| 1965 | 7-1-2 |
| 1966 | 4-5-1 |
| 1968 | 5-5-0 |
| 1969 | 5-5-0 |

His overall coaching record at Willingham High School was: 63-42-15.

In 1970, Billy Henderson joined Mount de Sales as assistant football coach under Mike Garvin and was the head baseball coach. The Cavaliers won two state championships in baseball under Henderson in 1971 and 1972, which led to him being named the National Baseball Coach of the Year in 1972.

**Clarke Central High School**

| | | |
|---|---|---|
| 1973 | 4-6 | |
| 1974 | 5-4-1 | |
| 1975 | 6-5 | Sub-Region Title |
| 1976 | 9-2 | Sub-Region Title |
| 1977 | 14-0 | State Championship |
| 1978 | 9-2 | Sub-Region Title |
| 1979 | 15-0 | State Championship |
| 1980 | 9-3 | Sub-Region Title |
| 1981 | 7-4-0 | |
| 1982 | 12-1 | Region Title |
| 1983 | 12-1 | Region Title |
| 1984 | 13-2 | North Georgia Championship |
| 1985 | 15-0 | State Championship |
| 1986 | 14-1 | North Georgia Championship |
| 1987 | 7-4 | |
| 1988 | 7-4 | |
| 1989 | 12-3 | North Georgia Championship |
| 1990 | 11-3 | Area Championship |
| 1991 | 10-3 | Region Championship |
| 1992 | 12-3 | North Georgia Championship |
| 1993 | 2-8 | |
| 1994 | 6-4 | |
| 1995 | 11-2 | Region Championship |

Coach Henderson was at Clarke Central for 23 years. He compiled a 222-65-1 record during that time. His teams won three state championships, seven North Georgia titles, twelve region crowns, and fourteen sub-region titles. They made nineteen playoff appearances and went to seven state championship games, including three in consecutive years, '84, '85, '86. He also saw 150 players receive college scholarships. Henderson's final coaching record for football was 286-107-15.

# ACKNOWLEDGEMENTS

Many people helped in the writing of this book. Some of these provided hands-on help while others gave loads of encouragement.

First and foremost, I wish to thank Billy Henderson. I met with him in Athens on many occasions at his well-known office at the Holiday Inn (across from the University of Georgia campus). His wonderful family really contributed much more than they will ever know. Carol, Chris, Fran, and Johnny, I want to take this opportunity to thank you for all that you've done to help in this process. Carol particularly spent many hours collecting pictures. I was in contact with her by e-mail many times, discussing interview scheduling as well as other pertinent things, and I appreciate her patience and positive attitude.

Thanks are in order to Catherine Staton and Dave Jones of Stroud & Hall Publishing Company.

I also wish to express appreciation to the staff at the Holiday Inn in Athens, who was always so cooperative with us. Special thanks go to Mike Waldrip, Vice President of Operations for the Holiday Inn.

Claude Felton and his staff at the University of Georgia Sports Communication Department provided information and photos, for which I am grateful.

My family provided much support and inspiration and put up with me constantly talking about this book. My son Stephen kept reminding me that I needed to write it. In the early stages when I was unsure of whether or not to do it, he relentlessly pushed me to pursue the goal. My wife Rosemary and my daughter Karen helped with research and provided the editing, which was no small chore. Their suggestions and attention to detail were invaluable. Stephen's wife Donna gave untold encouragement. To my two sisters, Margie and Dorothy, who shared my excitement about this endeavor, I say thanks. And, of course, my three grandsons, James, Sebastien, and Thomas make everything in my life more meaningful.

One special friend was John McBride, who made every trip with me to Athens for the interviews. He provided much encouragement, conversation, and the added humor that helps make things so much more enjoyable. He even told me on one occasion that he now knows more about Billy Henderson than he does his own family!

Jim Whalen, who taught at Willingham High School during the Henderson years, gave much encouragement and support. My appreciation goes out to him, Bill Eargle, and my other lunch group buddies, and to anyone else who added the needed encouragement.

Much gratitude goes to the people who provided hours of interviews and shared their personal experiences. They know who they are.

Finally, and most importantly, I give praise to Jesus Christ, in whom I place all my trust for everything about my life.

# CONTRIBUTORS

I am very appreciative of all those who contributed stories and thoughts about Coach Henderson.

Ethan Armentrout
John Barnette
Billy Beale
Charles Bellflower
Bob Berlin
Carol Henderson Brooks
Steve Brooks
Claudie Brown
Larry Brown
Bobby Bryant
Ed Defore
Derek Dooley
Vince Dooley
Larry Evans
Bill Falconer
Douglas Furney
Pete Gaines
Willie Green
Jimmy Hammond
Bryan Harris
Jim Bob Harris
Edgar Hatcher
Johnny Henderson
Fran Henderson Hobbs
James Holland
Fred Johnson
John Kasay
Brian Kemp
Hugh Laing
Sonny Perdue
David Perno
Chester Pierce
Dan Pitts
Charles Pledger
Alan Redmond
Johnny Stallings
Mike Waldrip
Chris Henderson Watts
Gary White
Ray Wilkes
Randy Williams

# INDEX